Joy Renewed

Joy Renewed

A Biblical Prescription for Rediscovering Joy in Late Modernity

BENJAMIN FISCHER
& CEDRIC KANANA

WIPF & STOCK • Eugene, Oregon

JOY RENEWED
A Biblical Prescription for Rediscovering Joy in Late Modernity

Copyright © 2021 Benjamin Fischer and Cedric Kanana. All rights reserved. Except for brief quotations in critical publications or reviews, no part of this book may be reproduced in any manner without prior written permission from the publisher. Write: Permissions, Wipf and Stock Publishers, 199 W. 8th Ave., Suite 3, Eugene, OR 97401.

Wipf & Stock
An Imprint of Wipf and Stock Publishers
199 W. 8th Ave., Suite 3
Eugene, OR 97401

www.wipfandstock.com

PAPERBACK ISBN: 978-1-6667-1556-9
HARDCOVER ISBN: 978-1-6667-1557-6
EBOOK ISBN: 978-1-6667-1558-3

JUNE 28, 2021

All Scripture quotations are from The ESV® Bible (The Holy Bible, English Standard Version®), copyright © 2001 by Crossway, a publishing ministry of Good News Publishers. Used by permission. All rights reserved.

Dedicated to Bishop Ngendahayo Emmanuel,

our brother and friend,

Who gives his life that others may find joy

Contents

Part I: Joy and Its Loss

1. Joy By Design: Remembering Our Story | 3
2. Disrupted Design: The Fall of Joy | 14
3. Getting Up to Speed: The Poverty of Modernity | 24

Part II: Paths to Rediscovering Joy

4. The Joy of Knowing God | 39
5. The Joy of Living God's Ways | 52
6. The Simple Joy of Contentment | 66
7. The Joy of Serving in the Kingdom | 79
8. The Joy of Agreeing with God: Confession | 92
9. The Joy of Fellowship | 106
10. The Path to Joy Includes Suffering | 120
11. The Joy of Sharing in the Suffering of Christ | 129

Bibliography | 139

PART I
Joy and Its Loss

1

Joy By Design: Remembering Our Story

JOY IS INSEPARABLE FROM the human story. But if we forget our story, we also lose the knowledge of how joy is meant to fit. In order for any people to know itself truly, remembering its story is essential.

Rehearsing stories has been part of human society throughout the ages. There is an old legend of the Germanic people called *Beowulf*, written down as a long poem by a forgotten Anglo-Saxon monk sometime in the tenth century. One way to understand the poem is that Beowulf is given as a model for the Anglo-Saxons of how a hero ought to live in faithfulness to God's design. As Beowulf comes into the ongoing story of his people, his special design quickly shows itself: he is very strong. Despite doing some foolish things with his strength (like a Germanic Samson), as the story gets moving, the man of strength and courage whom God has made him to be comes to meet the terrible needs of a moment. A monster is attacking and destroying a neighboring kingdom. So Beowulf comes and kills the marauding troll and then its avenging mother.

At the feast after his battles, the old king, Hrothgar, gives the young hero some advice. He reminds Beowulf that the Almighty

Part I: Joy and Its Loss

God apportions kingdoms. But it often happens that after a king has had great success—gaining wealth, victories, and health—he grows arrogant. Hrothgar cautions, "Now sleeps the watchman, guardian of his soul." Just then, the enemy of our souls "shoots arrows beneath his guard, so he is smitten to the heart with a bitter shaft. Too little now seems what he has enjoyed, his grim heart fills with greed, to him all joy is lost. Defend thee from that deadly malice, dear Beowulf, best of knights, and choose for thyself the better part, counsels of everlasting worth".[1] And Beowulf *does* choose the better part. He becomes king and rules fifty years, bringing his people into security and prosperity among the warring tribes. The story ends with him dying in battle, killing a dragon who comes to destroy his kingdom. He sacrifices himself for his people, and the Christian monk recording the legend gives the judgment: "That was a good king." Throughout the long poem, story after story is woven into Beowulf's legend to contrast him with other ancient Germanic kings who swerved off course, who took the way Hrothgar warned about and ignored "counsels of everlasting worth."

This story reminds us that wise people have always understood that the journey we take, and the significance of any given decision, depends on where we aim to get. We measure and assign value according to the ultimate end, what Aristotle called a *telos*. Until quite recently, it was assumed that we need stories and models to show us the best ends and how to get there. The stories of lives lived well are passed to the next generation so that the younger can come to understand what a good life looks like, lived out in its fullness, to its best end.

Even one generation ago, in the East Africa of my (Cedric) parents' youth, almost every night and every special occasion included the telling of stories. We have a proverb about these times: "A youth that does not cultivate friendship with the elderly is like a tree without roots." For us, cultivating friendship meant listening. Older people were guardians of our people's treasures, and through times of storytelling, they gifted them to eager young listeners. From one perspective, the stories connected us—the new

---

1. Tolkein, *Beowulf*, 64-5, lines 1459-75.

growth—to our roots. They told us what sort of tree we were part of, or what our nature is. From another perspective, they told us where we were going, or how to grow. We needed to know what was worthy of imitation. Without such stories—like the stories of Hrothgar and Beowulf for the Anglo-Saxons—without such paths presented for subsequent generations, the next generation of a society becomes wanderers in a trackless wilderness, as pleased to settle down at a mud-hole as at the River of Life.

The writer of the letter to the Hebrews shares this view about stories and their instructive value. The whole eleventh chapter contains at least eighteen reminders of how the Jewish ancestors had shown, through their lives, what faith in God looks like. Along with defining faith as "the assurance of things hoped for, the conviction of things not seen," Hebrews takes pains to show what it looks like when a person walks the way of faith. Noticeable in each and every case explicitly mentioned, as well as others alluded to, is that all the exemplars of faith encountered terrible difficulty. The road of faith is also the road of suffering. In case his hearers might miss the point, in the midst of recounting the deeds of the faithful, the writer says clearly in verses 13–16: "These all died in faith, not having received the things promised, but having seen them and greeted them from afar, and having acknowledged that they were strangers and exiles on the earth. For people who speak thus make it clear that they are seeking a homeland. If they had been thinking of that land from which they had gone out, they would have had opportunity to return. But as it is, they desire a better country, that is, a heavenly one. Therefore God is not ashamed to be called their God, for he has prepared for them a city." The writer wraps up the summary of these faithful people by saying, "They were stoned, they were sawn in two, they were killed with the sword. They went about in skins of sheep and goats, destitute, afflicted, mistreated— of whom the world was not worthy—wandering about in deserts and mountains, and in dens and caves of the earth. And all these, though commended through their faith, did not receive what was promised, since God had provided something better for us, that apart from us they should not be completed" (Heb 11:37–40).

Part I: Joy and Its Loss

There is a shocking paradox in his message, which is also one of the great paradoxes of the essential Christian message. God is calling people into this way filled with suffering and sense of exile, and the Bible is commending it as the good road, but from the short-term perspective it sounds pretty awful. This difficult way of the ancients' faith—very honestly told as the way of a stranger and exile—is somehow good. It is the *good road* because it takes us to the *good end*, to the place God has promised, to the homeland, the better country, the heavenly city.

Consider also what goes unstated. Everyone is traveling *some* road, and everyone is going to arrive at *some* destination. The journey itself shapes you according to where the road leads. If you are going to a mud-hole or the town dump, the journey prepares you for that end. If you are going to the great celebration, where rewards are given to each new arrival and honor is freely shared, the journey will shape you to receive rewards and share honor. That celebration, to which the ancients have already arrived, is not yet completed until all of us latecomers arrive.

Chapter 12 of Hebrews begins by gesturing to this end and to the journey we have to take. He compares it to a race. "Therefore, since we are surrounded by so great a cloud of witnesses, let us also lay aside every weight, and sin which clings so closely, and let us run with endurance the race that is set before us" (Heb 12:1). In numbers so great they are like a cloud, those who have completed their race await each of us to complete ours. They are not spectators—the root word *martyr* is not used for spectators or an audience; they are the crowd of those whose lives give testimony and tell about the kingdom course they have run. They are the ones who have overcome by the blood of the Lamb and the word of their testimony. As the church taught anciently and the Reformers agreed, the eyes of the departed are on the Lord himself as they await the full number for the resurrection.

So this surrounding or enveloping cloud of martyrs are all models and reminders of how we are to run this race. If we want to know how to run in faith, there is a crowd whose stories demonstrate it. They provide the stories and the modeled journey for the road we are on, so that we can see that the race can be run and the arduous effort can be done. And since we have these stories testifying to the way, "let us also," he says, "lay aside every weight, and sin which clings so closely, and let us run with endurance"—as they did—"the race marked out for us."

Moreover, Hebrews tells us we have an even better place to look, a better end and an even better model than provided by those faithful ancients. The whole book of Hebrews has the refrain of Jesus as the better one, the fulfillment of prophet, priest, and king. The same theme of completion is true here. As we run our course, we can look not only to exemplars of faith among the ancients of Israel, but we can look to the founder or originator, who is also the perfecter and completer of faith: Jesus, our great representative and brother.

THE JOY OF OUR FORERUNNER

Nothing will show us better how to think about the end to which we are going, or the way we go to get there, than to look at Jesus. None could more clearly show us the story we are in or how to live our place in it. Thus, we are told, "let us run with endurance the race that is set before us, looking to Jesus, the founder and perfecter of our faith, who for the joy that was set before him endured the cross, despising the shame, and is seated at the right hand of the throne of God" (Heb 12:1–2). In this well-known passage, Hebrews carries the notion of a model journey to its highest. Jesus is not only the Truth and the Life, but he is also the Way to get there and shows us how to follow him.

The end for which the forerunner Jesus ran was the joy set before him, the glorious condition he had left when he came among us as the Word made flesh. We get glimpses of his eternal glory in Philippians 2, Colossians 1, and the opening and concluding chapters of Revelation. The joy for which Jesus suffered and to which he was restored was being "in the form of God" and having "equality with God" (Phil 2:6), unfettered by the limitations of human flesh in his complete unity with the Father and Spirit. His joy was being perfectly known by Father and Spirit in every facet of himself, being the very "image of God" and the "radiance of the glory of God and the exact imprint of his nature," "for in him the fullness of God was pleased to dwell" (Heb 1:3 and Col 1:15, 19). This relationship describes unmediated, complete knowledge and perfect appreciation. Father, Son, and Holy Spirit had eternally shared the unique joy of perfectly knowing the infinite depths of one another and the delight of being perfectly known.

As he had been from eternity loved and glorified for everything that he is, when Jesus looked toward his suffering and death, he knew he would leave behind the mocking and scorn of his creatures and return to being rightly praised and honored. Along with again enjoying divine fellowship, his joy included his preeminence, ruling all things and uniting all things by his rule, and being rightly and joyously worshiped and loved for his goodness. "For by him all things were created, in heaven and on earth, visible and invisible, whether thrones or dominions or rulers or authorities—all things were created through him and for him" (Col 1:16). Whereas in the towns of Galilee and on the streets of Jerusalem he endured the sorrows of rejection from his beloved, he looked ahead to the song of the Lamb: "Great and amazing are your deeds, O Lord God the Almighty! Just and true are your ways, O King of the nations! Who will not fear, O Lord, and glorify your name? For you alone are holy" (Rev 15:3–4). It was the joy of fullness to which he looked. Everything made right.

This restoration of all things is also the end or goal to which we have been re-made to look. Jesus is our forerunner, who opened the way through death so we can run to that same end of everything restored to rights. He has turned our tragic story into a divine comedy, complete with a wedding at the end.

JOY IN PARADISE

The joy of Jesus from all eternity and that which was set before him as he endured the cross demonstrates the essence of joy in its highest expression. Of course, the experience of the Almighty is beyond the grasp of our understanding, just as the quality of his joy is infinitely great. But the doctrine of humanity made in the image of God can help us move from the highest to our own designed participation. In the Eden given to Adam and Eve, the divine image-bearing humans lived with an imitating joy proper and fitting to their created capacities. Exploring this designed participation is a good place to start as we begin this reflection on joy.

In Paradise, joy as we have seen it in the fulfillment of Jesus's mission was also part of the everyday life of Adam and Eve. Still filled with the Logos and united to him, the divine Word conveyed true knowledge of God, self, each other, and creation.[2] With true knowledge as their guide for relating, Adam and Eve must be described as, by design, relating properly to all things. Objectively, this state has often been described as the Hebrew *shalom*, or peace in its fullness.[3] Subjectively, this state of perfect relating conveys the feeling of joy. Let's consider in more detail.

With the indwelling Word speaking and teaching about the character of their Creator and Father, the unfallen ones were on a steady course of discovery. As Richard Hooker long ago explained in *The Laws of Ecclesiastical Polity*, humans have ever known about God only those facets of himself that he has chosen to reveal. This was as true of Adam and Eve as of Abraham, Moses, David, down to the apostles and throughout the Christian age. Steadily strengthening their fleshly capacity to hold more and more knowledge of his divine nature, the Creator led Adam and Eve in the joy of moving deeper and deeper into his glory. Think of the wonder! Each day was necessarily better than the one before because each one was enriched by knowing God more.

Another facet of the experience was their nakedness of soul before God, an idea brought into the visible by their physical nakedness. Having been created by God and moment by moment living in the knowledge of his Word and in accordance with him,

---

2. This incipient design and loss of the Logos of God is nowhere so well described as by Athanasius in *On the Incarnation*.

3. A thorough discussion of the biblical shalom can be found in Graham Cole's *God the Peacemaker*.

Part I: Joy and Its Loss

they never entertained the absurdity of hiding thoughts from him. Their thoughts were unfiltered. Intuition flowing from the Word found full and constant acceptance in their reason. Constantly submitted to the Word, what seemed right and good was actually right and good. Consequently, with nothing to hide—nor even having the notion of concealing or deceit—there was no shadow or hint of shame in their consciousness. This full and constant openness and disclosure before God, an innocent nakedness of soul, was the design.

We can say, then, that they were conscious of being fully known and absolutely delighted in by their Creator, reminiscent of the relationship of the Trinity whose image they bore. As they exercised their reason and moved about in Paradise, making discoveries about the Creation and the Creator, they found and felt the pleasure of God's delight in them. They were acting according to design. They lived with the smile of God upon them. Subjectively, what they felt is what we describe with the word "joy," both flowing from God and from knowing that they were pleasing the one worthy of being pleased.

Their own experience of one another brought another aspect to their participation in joy. Paul explains in Ephesians 5 how the marriage of a man and woman reveals mysteries of God's love; likewise, the design of marriage in Paradise demonstrates how human relationships were made to be part of participation in the joy of God. Adam and Eve were naked before God in body and soul, and they were also naked to one another. Similar to their relating to God, neither had thoughts or inclinations to hide from the other. Living without shame but with complete openness to each other, their physical nakedness represented their full self-disclosure. Adam's thoughts were fully shared with a fascinated Eve; her feelings were fully shared with an interested Adam. The world was all before them, and the fun of its discovery together enriched each new moment. As each one grew in self-understanding, in the knowledge of God, and in wisdom about the world, they shared their thrill of deepening in the participation of the Creator and Creation.

Joy By Design: Remembering Our Story

As we have all felt on occasion, to share something new with one we love brings joy. The excitement of the experience turns to exhilaration of mutual partaking in it, a sudden recognition that the same truth has dawned on us both.[4] We look with flashing eyes at each other and know that words will fail, but we often stumble excitedly through a gush of syllables, wanting to prolong the shared joy. So while any new truth is wonderful to see even alone, sharing that knowledge with another makes the wonder so much greater. This, too, was part of our design, that our joy could reach heights together that it could never reach alone.

Part of the designed sharing of Adam and Eve included not only discovery but also the pleasure of work and service. In Paradise God gave the first parents the task of stewarding and cultivating his own Creation. Sometimes this task has been interpreted merely as a matter of mutual benefit to earth and humanity. Indeed, the indwelling Word gave Adam and Eve right understanding of the world. When Adam named the animals, he imitated his Creator by speaking the nature of things.[5] When God spoke the nature of things, they came into existence. When Adam spoke their nature, he echoed and imitated God, re-establishing God's relationship to them through his vice-regent, and all the animals' roles relative to one another. Likewise, when the couple cultivated the Garden, rightly keeping in trust what had been given to them to order, they ordered it according to the wisdom coming from the Word. This order, as this interpretation implies, was for the good of the earth and the good of humanity, producing health for all.

This picture is again one of shalom in a rightly ordered world filled with the rule of God. But for our purposes it is also worth saying that the work given in Paradise also indicates another designed source of joy. Work and worthy service not only please and give health, but they also bring joy. Undoubtedly, Adam and Eve

---

4. C.S. Lewis's description of the origin of friendship in *The Four Loves* mirrors this surprise at finding another person who shares the same truth about something.

5. Walter Benjamin's essay "On Language as Such" provides helpful insight into the nature of Man in his imitative capacity as one who names.

Part I: Joy and Its Loss

divided their labors in the Garden according to their individual pleasure and skill—a shared end with unique tasks. Working together in complementary labor, the contributions of each were highlighted and celebrated. Through each one's limitations, they came to appreciate the other's abilities, growing in deeper appreciation for one another as time and experience taught, and as the indwelling Word showed them.

With their complementarity guided by the growing wisdom given from God, they were able to accomplish their service to their Creator. The joy of approval, so wonderful when given singularly, was multiplied by their cooperative service. Like children running to a smiling parent, Adam and Eve could gleefully skip to their Lord, eager to present their work to him. With no sense of scarcity and no notion of limited good, their only competition would be to praise the contribution of the other. Every comment brought more joy—the pleasure of giving praise and the honor of receiving it.

Finally, we can surmise a certain paradisal joy of self-knowledge in Adam and Eve deriving from the indwelling Word and from unfettered relationship with each other. So enraptured by the wonder of God, the mystery of the other person, and the unfolding interest of the Creation, self-forgetfulness was perhaps their norm. Each one came to self-knowledge by way of comprehending his and her own role in the created order. God had begun relationship with humans, as well as their relationship with Creation, so he set the terms for ongoing life together. As Adam and Eve followed the lead of the indwelling Word, each came to understand himself and herself in terms of participation in life together.

We could say they came to self-knowledge through roles—child of God, husband, wife, keeper of earth, gardener with this or that ability. The roles were generic to being a male or female human but also specific to each one's unique personal design. To live these roles was peace. But to live them also brought the particular taste of joy we commonly associate with contentment. It is the joy of neither having nor wanting more or other than is good and fitting. It is a joy especially connected to accurate self-knowledge. In Paradise, perfect self-knowledge came through continuing depth of relationship to God, companion, and creation. Ever deepening, but fixed according to the roles as established by God. To recognize, appreciate, and marvel at one's own unique design within the complex creation was a source of unending and ever-deepening joy.

Thus we speculate on the joy of Paradise before the Fall of humanity. We find it was more or less a wonderful byproduct of right choices made according to the light of love-filled reason. As Adam and Eve lived out their design, obediently following the leading of the indwelling Word, their subjective experience was shot through with joy. In sum, participating in the peace and love of God, as part of a world and kingdom oriented towards God and ordered rightly with respect to one another, produced joy. With love as the motive for action and peace as the resulting state of affairs, joy is the feeling of such a life. This was God's design.

QUESTIONS FOR REFLECTION

What stories other than God's biblical story have shaped your life and how you think about what is important? How do these stories agree with the biblical story or lead away from it?

What part of his joy in the heavenlies do you think was most absent during Jesus's earthly life?

In the account of joy in Paradise, what aspects of the good design sound most pleasant to you? Why do you think you most desire those particular aspects?

2

Disrupted Design: The Fall of Joy

IN 2014, I (CEDRIC) began visiting Kigali Central Prison to preach and offer pastoral care, becoming a chaplain there in 2015. Visiting weekly, I found myself encountering what seemed like all the ways God's good design could be corrupted. One week, I might preach to a group who had taken part in the Genocide, killing their neighbors simply for being part of a different ethnic group, or because local leaders told them to and they feared to disobey. Another time I might hold prayer with a convicted drug dealer, a child abuser, a thief, and someone deemed threatening to the government. Some were falsely accused. There were men suffering from alcohol withdrawals and men who had totally lost their minds. There were Pentecostals and Protestants, Catholics, Muslims, worshippers of many gods and worshippers only of self. All of them were miserable, hungry, sad, and lonely. There are few places where the outworking of human sin could be more glaring, or where despair holds sway with such ruthlessness. And yet, we know it is a scene repeated countlessly in prisons around the world.

Something has gone wrong. All is *not* right with the world. Everyone everywhere knows it, and overcoming the endless obstacles to human happiness—whether conceived religiously,

Disrupted Design: The Fall of Joy

philosophically, socially, physically, or emotionally—has been a driving force of intellectual activity for millennia. From the founts of philosophy in ancient Greece, to the Roman genius for administrative order, to the medieval passion for synthesis and organizational social structure, and to the modern obsession with science, every society spends its greatest energies to avoid being overwhelmed by a sense of meaninglessness and by the accompanying desperate attempts to silence it. Kigali Central Prison is not unique in its joylessness and creative invention of evil.

All these outworkings of desperation are traceable to an essential deficit in humanity, a deficit not part of the design but introduced as a corruption of it. With an act of disobedience, God's good design for joyful life was thwarted in every facet.

From its earliest days, Christianity has explained the loss of joy in connection with the Fall of Adam and Eve. Perfect in design as discussed in chapter 1, our Great Parents experienced ongoing and deepening joy through the indwelling Word of God and the accompanying unity with God and each other. But as created beings, their lives were always contingent. That is, their design depended upon God's ongoing sustaining power, and their enjoyment depended upon obedience to what God had directed and to what the indwelling Word prompted. Goodness, life, and joy were inextricably bound up with choices made in accord with God's words spoken to them and God's inwardly speaking Word. Even the simple matter of eating from almost any tree in God's garden brought affirmation and delight because it was a perfectly right choice. Yet, through aggressive temptation from Satan, they were given a false word: the suggestion of a wrong choice and the imagination of something being withheld. This false word was not something they would have imagined on their own as a potential good. It had to come to them from an external source, one suggesting that the wrong choice was a good one. They chose the false word, a message of independence from God.

In the unraveling consequences of this rebellion, one of the chief victims was joy. Every aspect of human life that was designed to bring joy inevitably brought related forms of suffering. Almost immediately after rejecting God's word to them, Adam and Eve began to experience suffering as deprivation, as isolation, as confusion and error, and as hostility.

LOSING THE WORD OF GOD

Because God's Word could not dwell in the corrupted human spirit, humans lost the unfettered, intimate knowledge of God they had been enjoying. Cut off from the Word meant being cut off from the source of life and all the goodness directly flowing from him. Choosing the false word of Satan alienated people from God by accepting Satan's view of all things, becoming oriented to his enslaving kingdom, his tyrannous rule, and his condemnation. We often call this "fallenness," and it is the fountain of all our suffering.

Foremost, fallen humans no longer have an uncorrupted understanding of the Almighty God. Choosing not to obey him, we lost knowledge of who he is, so that the outworking of Satan's false word was a wrong view of God in endless variety: as unkind, grasping, merciless, selfish, mean, old, capricious, inaccessible, and angry—essentially, any and all of the ways the petty gods of the nations have been imagined. The images of God as a kindly old man, or a violent dad, or even as a sentimental grandmother indicate our loss of knowledge and terrible willingness to think about him in whatever way seems to satisfy a psychological need. Losing the Word of God in us has meant always thinking about God through a corrupted lens.

The shape of our corrupted view of God tends to be driven by a related deprivation—the feeling of being unknown. By design, we experienced the joy of exploring God and his world within the security of his goodwill and the comfortable assurance that he would deal with us according to our slender capacities. He knew how much newness we could handle, while we knew he would supply each and every need. But with a corrupted view of God, instead of the constant assurance and security coming from intimate connection with the Creator, fallen humans are fundamentally driven by need and the fear that those needs will not be met.

Disrupted Design: The Fall of Joy

In Paradise, the indwelling Word of God spoke the right understanding of every experience, but in a fallen life without true knowledge, we interpret through Satan's lens of scarcity and competition.

THE STATE OF INSURRECTION

One of the most common ways the early church explained the fallen condition was that a fundamental change had occurred in wisdom. They often made contrasts between two ways of being and living, or two opposed kinds of wisdom. The letter of James is of course the most well known articulation.[1] James contrasts "wisdom from above," which is "first pure, then peaceable, gentle, open to reason, full of mercy and good fruits, impartial and sincere," with another wisdom, which is "earthly, unspiritual, demonic" and produces "bitter jealousy and selfish ambition in your hearts" (Jas 3:14–17). Intimately connected with the eternal Word of God, the Jewish notion of the wisdom of God was a way of talking about the knowledge that had been lost and had been displaced by worldly wisdom.

Etymology provides a helpful hint to understand how joy and suffering are linked to the two wisdoms. The Greek for wisdom in the New Testament is *sophia*, while early Latin translations of the New Testament give *sapientia*, the root being *sapia*. So, *sophia* and *sapia*. Together, these words for wisdom tell us that the foundational concept behind these terms was expressed by a common Indo-European root (Indo-European being the mother language from which Greek and Latin both derived): *sapio*, meaning "tasting or perceiving." In other words, these respective languages help us see James's special point about the Two Ways. The two wisdoms are two different ways of *perceiving* life. Every moment, every bit of our experience can be perceived according to different authorities with their own sets of assumptions. As we have seen, we were

---

1. Other well-known examples of the Two Ways are from the second-century *Didache* and its contemporary *Epistle of Barnabas*, along with the later *Apostolic Constitutions*.

designed to perceive according to true knowledge coming from God, but in a fallen condition, we have accepted a whole different mode of perception.

James describes the consequences of Satan's wisdom in 4:1–4. Lacking the governance of God's indwelling Word, it is a state of war *within* the self, leading to contention *between* people. "What causes quarrels and what causes fights among you? Is it not this, that your passions are at war *within* you?" According to the wisdom of the Fall, our various passions and impulses jockey for authoritative position, for the right to determine our decisions. It is as Brutus argued with himself in Shakespeare's *Julius Caesar*: "The [spirit] and the mortal instruments / are then in council, and the state of a man / like to a little kingdom, suffers then / the nature of an insurrection" (Act II.i.66–69).[2] Competing desires are typically irreconcilable. James's Greek word for these competing self-focused passions, desires, or lusts is *hedonon*, the concept on which the Hedonists based their view of life. Their whole way of being and mode of perception was to surrender to passions and the pursuit of pleasure. Stoics like Brutus, on the other hand, sought to resolve the inner war by harnessing and bringing the passions into subjection, arguing that basic fleshly impulses cloud higher, abstract virtues.

What is common among the many expressions of unspiritual wisdom is that every goal and all the points of reference, even the abstract virtues, are understood to belong to a perishing order. That is, they are disconnected from the everlasting rule of God and carry the assumption of no eternal life. In Augustine's *City of God*, he describes this approach to life as the "earthly city" or the "city of man," suggesting the totalizing system of thought when man is disconnected from God. "We see then that the two cities were created by two kinds of love: the earthly city was created by self-love reaching the point of contempt for God, the Heavenly City by the love

---

2. Shakespeare's phrase is "the Genius and the mortal instruments…" In late sixteenth-century England, the word "Genius" meant a person's unique spirit.

of God carried as far as contempt of self."[3] Those who perceive life according to the assumptions of a perishing order naturally and even reasonably yield to selfish passions. Indeed, if this is all there is, they ought to be self-focused. If our existence truly is short, then "Eat, drink and be merry, for tomorrow we die." The bottom line is that according to unspiritual wisdom—the little candle that every society lights for itself in the fallen age—death is the ultimate fact. Death is the rarely-spoken, never-acknowledged motivator, and the darkness that sends people rushing to what little light they can kindle together.

Of course, the consequences of life shadowed by fear of death parade themselves before us every day. The cultural and political leaders of every society graphically demonstrate the kinds of choices that are made when the normal limitations of money, power, and ability are removed. Hollywood movie stars move from marriage to marriage, drug-scandal to abuse-scandal. Presidents and prime ministers destroy their families while scorning any pretense at morality. The recent #MeToo movement helpfully served to reveal the shocking extent to which men with power and wealth believe themselves to be above the law of the land, not to mention the ways of God. Notwithstanding the obvious wickedness, the logic of the death-formed life fails to provide real accountability for evil. According to its logic, there is no inherent evil, only the unwelcome transgression of another's boundaries. It cannot be considered evil, just illegal. With national leaders, television, and film providing models of unbridled self-indulgence to the degree that the law will allow, we have plenty of illustration of Paul's description of the earthly city: "Their end is destruction, their god is their belly, and they glory in their shame, with minds set on earthly things" (Phil 3:19).

With death as the looming finality and a filter on all perception, then goals and potential goods are all necessarily short-term and calculated to maximize pleasure for the self. As James suggests by the "passions at war within you," there is a competition of stimuli *within* the self — a person responds and reasons about what to

---

3. Augustine, *The City of God*, 14:28.

Part I: Joy and Its Loss

pursue by quick evaluations of what will give most pleasure, most immediately. And in societies filled with people inwardly torn by these death-fearing, pleasure-aiming calculations, contention and jealousy flow naturally and unavoidably.

Guided by a perception of death's finality, one of the common conclusions has been that a life that loses pleasure and short-term good is a life without meaning and certainly without joy. Shakespeare's Prince Hamlet betrays this calculation in his famous "To be or not to be" soliloquy, inwardly debating "Whether 'tis nobler in the mind to suffer / the slings and arrows of outrageous fortune, / or to take arms against a sea of troubles, / And by opposing end them? To die: to sleep" (Act 3.i.58–61). Shakespeare recognized the timelessness of this form of reasoning. Sometime in the 1590s, Shakespeare had read the newly translated sermons on Matthew of the fourth-century Bishop of Constantinople, John Chrysostom. He was captivated by Chrysostom's teaching on the misery of the fallen world. Preaching about the courage of suffering Christians, Chrysostom contrasted their courage with the desperation of those who ignore eternity. Who could "look at the things here, at those in the prisons, those in the mines, those on the dunghills, the possessed, the frantic, them that are struggling with incurable diseases, those that are fighting against continual poverty, them that live in famine, them that are pierced with irremediable woes, those in captivity ... How shall we bear it? ... Who would suffer these things here, unless vengeance and punishments were to await all?"[4] He might as well have been describing Kigali Prison. In Chrysostom's hypothetical sufferer, Shakespeare heard the reasoning that had become increasingly common in his own day—in the era that the word "atheist" first entered the English language. Both Chrysostom and Shakespeare understood that without eternal life in view, death becomes the supreme fact for a short life without joy.

Satan introduced this way of perceiving and this fallen wisdom into God's good creation. It is his own perception because he is also subject to it. Having lost everlasting life with God, the fallen powers know their time is limited. Despite the bitter hostility of

---

4. Chrysostom, "Homily 76," 461.

Disrupted Design: The Fall of Joy

their rebellion and the immeasurable intensity of their hate, their powers are checked, as Christ "disarmed the rulers and authorities and put them to open shame, triumphing over them" (Col 2:15). After the cross of Jesus, they have only the power of lies and the fear of death to wield. The goals of their fallen kingdom are to sow fear and to capture people in the logic of death and in perceiving according to the bodily passions. As long as humans perceive and act according to the fear of death, they continue to live under the rule and rubrics of the fallen powers, remaining alienated from God. In the arsenal of evil, one of the most powerful weapons for capturing or maintaining people in the fear of death is suffering.

If joy describes the subjective experience of living with God according to his design, as we suggested in chapter 1, then suffering is a shorthand way to describe the subjective experience of encountering discordance with his design—in relationship to the self, others, and creation. Relating to others and making decisions according to unspiritual wisdom, with death as the ultimate reality, humans are deprived of joy. Instead, when people are controlled by fear, a sense of scarcity, and belief in limited good, suffering has a predominant place in the subjective experience of humankind.

As the normal outlook of people all over the world, this common experience of fear and scarcity generally simmers within each human heart. But even a glance at history reveals that sometimes social and environmental conditions create a moment when segments of a community or country identify a common enemy, and the internal warfare spills out. Satan's view of life becomes an ideology, a complete way of viewing all of life according to a single principle. To our great grief, we in Rwanda know it too well. Through the time of our subjugation to Belgian colonization, the sense of limited good and honor began to shape our national thinking. Driven into thinking tribally, we lost our national story of being one Rwandan people and began to believe the racialized story of irreconcilable differences brought to us from Europe. The same poisonous spring that gave rise to Nazism fed tribalism in Africa. After independence, segments of our society increasingly adopted Satan's view of scarcity, believing that limited good meant we had to seize what we could for our own family and tribe. In 1994, as the world knows, the simmering desperation for dominance erupted in ethnic violence as one group sought to completely kill off another group. Almost a million people were reduced to less than animals in the eyes of their killers. Those who lived through that time remember how Satan's thinking shaped all public conversation. Certain of limited good, some had to die. Fear of death and its ultimacy reigned over everything.

While we wish it were unique, Rwanda's experience typifies what has commonly happened through history and continues to occur throughout the world. I (Cedric) have been deeply disturbed in visits to America over the last few years because I have heard the same rhetoric in the mouths of ideological Democrats and Republicans as we heard before the Genocide of 1994. The language of hate that reduces our political enemies to the level of dangerous insanity or beasts is Satan's ploy to fuel fear, and his reeking breath is animating much of what passes for political discourse in America today. Uncertain situations like the coronavirus pandemic only fuel the passions already present. If death lurks with absolute authority on the horizon, so Satan whispers, then we must eliminate our dangerous rivals so that our own kind can survive as long as possible. Fear, danger, scarcity, threat, and death. When these messages dominate, the rule of God is ignored and there can be no joy.

QUESTIONS FOR REFLECTION

What do you think it would have felt like for Adam and Eve to lose the Word of God inside them when they rejected God's command? Do we ever feel anything similar?

As you think about the Two Ways, the way of life and the way of death, what decisions do you regularly make that are driven by the way of death? How do fears of scarcity, loss, and shortness of time factor into your thinking and choices?

Disrupted Design: The Fall of Joy

In your life, what area feels most touched by the Fall and the claims of death? What might it look and feel like if God's design were restored in that area?

3

Getting Up to Speed: The Poverty of Modernity

PREMODERN AND MODERN

SUFFERING IS A THOROUGHGOING part of life no matter where you live. In the shadowlands of earth, still held captive by the condemned powers of darkness, the lie of ultimate death maintains its hold and binds people in fear. And as we all know, of course, the sentence of the Fall continues to work itself out in creation—most noticeably in our mortal bodies. We suffer in body and in soul regardless of where we live on this earth.

And yet, depending on when and where a person lives, there are distinct forms of suffering that tend to mark the typical experience of life in that place. Is it a pre-modern society or a modern one? Is it a communal culture or an individualistic one? How much personal freedom is allowed by the government? How much is spiritual life a part of everyday thinking? Is personhood understood as primarily psychological, or as integrated mind, body, and soul? All these factors shape the way suffering takes shapes and is articulated. Going hand in hand with the culturally specific forms of suffering are also accompanying efforts to suppress it.

Getting Up to Speed: The Poverty of Modernity

Because dying is a part of life everywhere, the circumstances surrounding typical death can provide an interesting indicator and clue to how a society approaches suffering. As I (Ben) serve congregants approaching their own death or families who are losing a loved one, I often see them fighting against a common scenario in the modern West. Dying tends to happen in a hospital or nursing home, and many die alone. Overwhelmed by the care required for the aged or else too busy to be involved, many families give their elders to the care of professionals while quietly exiting from the scene. Sometimes relationally alienated, sometimes living far from relatives, the isolated elderly spend their final days under the occasional observation of medical staff. The moment of passing frequently goes unmarked.

More troubling still is the scenario of a natural death that remains undiscovered for days. Extreme cases illustrate the point, like that of Joyce Vincent, a well-educated and attractive 38-year old woman whose body decayed for three years in her London flat, TV still flickering.[1] In Japan, as modern as any country in the world, 30,000 people *every year* have "lonely deaths," what they call *kodokushi*, dying in their homes and remaining undiscovered for days or weeks.[2] Whether these extreme versions or the more common death in a nursing home, the idea of an isolated passing haunts many families and aging individuals. It was one of the terrors of efforts to contain the coronavirus in 2020. This is the scenario nobody wants for themselves, nor wants to be guilty of towards a family member. So we often find ourselves struggling to create situations in which a passing can be witnessed without being too disruptive to the family's normal functioning. Sadly, because our caregiving norms tend to isolate the aged, even people with involved families often die alone.

Then comes the grieving, and Americans especially find ourselves baffled. Because American culture has been formed through numerous strains of migration and cultural influence, there is no

---

1. The tragic story of Joyce Vincent is featured in *Dreams of a Life* (2011), written and directed by Carol Morley.
2. See Onshi, "A Generation," 2017; and Martin, "One diorama," 2019.

single common way for Americans to grieve or to show support for the grieving. Instead, we are trapped in a web of mixed messages. Our Christian heritage teaches us to "mourn with those who mourn," and many of the cultures informing our society have traditions of group comfort. Wakes and vigils appear throughout American literature from Hawthorne to Faulkner, and those practices continue strongly in some pockets. On the other hand, we are also influenced by a Germanic reserve and a Scots-Irish independent spirit. These cultural strains demand that people appear emotionally strong. We are in a bind. Neither wanting to show our own weakness, nor wanting to imply that others are weak or in need, we often assume grieving people want to be left alone. The contrary impulses create a common impasse—we want to comfort the grieving but feel constrained from doing so. A compromise between the community vigil and the stiff upper lip tends to be supplying meals for a few weeks, often timidly brought and gingerly left. As in death, so in grieving: Americans tend to grieve quiet and alone.

In sharp contrast, my (Cedric's) experience suggests that typical dying in East Africa might best be described as a communal rite. A person whose whole identity is connected in a web of interconnected relationships to their extended family and community also passes this life in company. We have a proverb that expresses it: "He who owns calamity eats it with his family." By this, we basically mean that suffering is shared, and even if a person gets into trouble on their own, it becomes the pain of the community. In normal times Africans are rarely alone, even in their own homes; much more so in times of crisis. If a man becomes seriously ill, all his siblings and the siblings of his spouse, cousins, friends, and neighbors will come to pay respect. The notion that the man might die alone is never even entertained. Instead, the effort is to comfort the spouse and children. Not only do people rarely die alone, they also tend to die at home, as we have done for centuries. It is true that the increase in hospitals and medical technology has increased the occurrence of people dying in hospitals, but everyone's preference is that a dying person be allowed to return home.

Getting Up to Speed: The Poverty of Modernity

In grief and mourning, Rwandans display the same tendency towards community. Upon news of a death, family and friends will travel hundreds of miles to be with the grieving family. Even small mud-brick houses—and the houses of neighbors—will be filled with visitors, sleeping on the floor for several weeks. The assumption is that no one should bear their grief alone, and grieving takes time. Some visitors will live with the bereaved for a month, and someone will be with the family at all times for the next year. Traditionally, soon after burial there is also a structured time in which those who knew the deceased can speak about any unfinished business, as various as unresolved conflict to outstanding debts. Everyone understands that the passing of this person has affected the entire community, and while the loss is especially keen for spouse and children, the loss changes every chain of connection in which that person was linked.

These differences in death and grieving between East Africa and the West demonstrate a general pattern of different dealing with suffering between pre-modern and modern cultures. Both pre-modern and modern societies are profoundly affected by the Fall, the loss of joy, and the prevalence of suffering. Both suffer physically, emotionally, mentally, and spiritually. Notwithstanding the fundamental commonalities, there are major differences in the ways that the respective societies try to cope with suffering. These attempts, and their relative success and failure, can help us as Christians to understand some common tendencies that hinder our pursuit of joy and unfortunately contribute to our suffering. Ultimately, pre-modern cultures assume the interconnectivity of lives—and the experience of joy and suffering—while modern cultures assume that individual lives connect only on the basis of choice.

SENSE OF SELF: PRE-MODERN TO MODERN

Western culture has not always been individualistic. Western society used to be as communal as African or Asian. A brief background to what happened in European society can help illustrate what exactly has been lost in the West but has been retained in much of the world, although the shift is powerfully underway in developing countries. In particular, the shift is most noticeable in how a person thinks of the self.

As Alisdair MacIntyre has shown in *After Virtue*, in premodern Western society people understood themselves in fixed ways. The question, "Who am I?" was very easily answered. A premodern European might have said, I am a member of a family (child of these parents, sibling to these boys and girls), who are descended from certain ancestors. Our heritage links us in unbreakable ways to others sharing that ancestry, giving us a known place within our village and broader people group. Our village has a known place within our nation, who worships a certain god or gods among many, or the Almighty God. In my family and village, I serve this people and this God or gods by performing a set of known functions. All of these strands of connection form a strong web of belonging, relationship, and purpose. As MacIntyre articulates, "I inherit from the past of my family, my city, my tribe, my nation, a variety of debts, inheritances, rightful expectations and obligations. These constitute the given of my life, my moral starting point."[3] In other words, stability of identity was established from every trajectory, through every role and relationship.

The related question, "What is a good life?" or "What is right?" was also very easily answered because it corresponded to all the answers of "Who am I?" What was good and right was always and already determined by custom—the inherited and ever-connected interrelationship of nation, religion, family practice, and local law handed on as the traditions of a people. Traditions that established shared customs produced an ongoing moral consensus, a thorough agreement about right and wrong, with a range of stated and implied expectations for every member of society. Regardless of one's place in society, a person never needed to wonder what was right for their role or a given decision within that role. He might have pondered why God or the gods had established a norm, and he might even have deviated from a sanctioned way, but he

---

3. MacIntyre, *After Virtue*, 220.

Getting Up to Speed: The Poverty of Modernity

understood the act as transgressive and wrong. The authority of custom was assumed.

While nobody wants to go back to pre-modern dentistry or internal medicine, what pre-modern society had going for it was stability of the self. Yes, people were concerned about survival, but they were never concerned about losing themselves or struggling with identity issues. When Jesus says in Matthew 6, "do not worry about your life" and "do not worry about tomorrow," he is talking about worries and anxieties for enough food to eat and not freezing to death. These were concerns of the body. In that context he was not talking about being properly valued, self-actualized, or affirmed in your choices. Those are modern problems. In the New Testament, God's call came to people with stable, fixed identities. So what happened?

Arguably, the major influence that began the Western shift towards modernity was the Black Death of the fourteenth century. Beginning in 1347, a combination of bubonic and pneumonic plague came from Asia and swept across Europe, killing at least a third of the population. Coming on the heels of serious flooding, a drop in average global temperature (sometimes called a mini Ice Age), famine, war across Europe, and a major earthquake in 1347, it was not surprising that Christians across the continent were expecting the end of the world. When deaths from famine and war are added to plague deaths, estimates of total population loss often approach one half the total European population of 1300. At the least, everyone understood the crisis spiritually, as God's judgment on his wayward people.

And judgment seemed to be warranted. Having a corporate identity, each nation and people group understood its members as occupying fixed roles and responsibilities within a "body politic," such that the overall health of society depended on each person rightly performing their role.[4] The king, as head, and nobility as arms should guard and protect the people from external danger and internal crime. The peasantry, as legs, should work to raise

---

4. The clearest articulation of this pre-modern notion was provided by the twelfth-century bishop John of Salisbury in his *Policraticus*.

Part I: Joy and Its Loss

the food for everyone and provide for the material needs. And the clergy (including priests, monks, and nuns) filled the whole body like a soul, praying and safeguarding the spiritual health of the people. With rampant corruption and public sin among the clergy, and a Bible no longer accessible to the common people, Christendom's crisis of the fourteenth century was almost universally interpreted as judgment on the church and its leaders for failing to live righteously. Like a corrupted soul, their failure meant the corruption of the whole people.

The terrible judgments shook up confidence in the authority of the church and all the traditions the people had inherited. Beginning motions of reflection and critique that led eventually to the Reformation, the crisis also introduced social mobility. With major labor shortages across the continent, as well as holes in the church hierarchy, peasants and especially skilled workers could charge for their labor for the first time and even enter the ranks of the learned. Rather than remaining tied to feudal estates, they could move to a new village or to a town. For the first time since the Germanic tribes settled in the Roman Empire, common people experienced both geographic and social mobility.

A key result was that mobility came at the cost of stability. That seems obvious, but the implications are not so easily seen. With the growth of cities in early modernity, people left their villages, just as is happening today all over Africa, Asia, and Latin America. They left home, family, the place of their ancestors, their community of worshipers, the practices that gave meaning to times and seasons and everyday life—the interrelationships of people, place, and practices that made life worth living. Sometimes they were escaping dangerous situations. But most often, the young got wind of prosperity or possibilities not available in their rural situations. When they arrived in the city, one of two things happened. Some found their own people there: others from their own background who shared their customs and view of life. In enclaves and ghettos, they reestablished the webs of meaning that gave identity to each person. The majority, though, lost themselves. The story of modernity includes the severing of incalculable strands that told young

Getting Up to Speed: The Poverty of Modernity

men and women who they were and what made life meaningful. They lost their stories. In this latter situation, the untethered individual joined with a crowd of others equally lost.

As this urbanization process intertwined with a rejection of the past, the emerging individual of early modernity (or the Renaissance, if you prefer) found a radical new freedom from traditional sources of authority—from family, church, and customary law. If "Who am I?" was no longer answered by the web of relationships or by the assumptions of received authority, the answer became a matter of invention. *I can be anyone.* Not constrained by the customs and inherited norms of village and small town, people experienced a dizzying array of possibilities for work, leisure, family, and eventually church. But if I can be anyone, I can also be no one.

While the Reformation left biblical authority intact, with God still assumed to be ruling, the climate of skepticism and the turn to a man-centered world received a significant philosophical boost in the seventeenth century. In 1637, Rene Descartes explained in his *Discourse On Method* that he had arrived at a new approach to being in the world, a new method of knowing not reliant on revelation or tradition: "I entirely abandoned the study of letters. Resolving to seek no knowledge other than that of which could be found in myself or else in the great book of the world."[5] He concluded with a short summation of the starting place: *Cogito ergo sum*, or "I think, therefore I am."[6] In short form, Descartes gave articulation to the modern mode of thought that has come to predominate in our society. Though never denying God's existence, Descartes set down the philosophical foundation that what we think or experience is the only truth one can depend on. To be fully alive and a thinker, one must begin with the self and reason from the self. It was a new formulation of an age-old tendency. With seeming philosophical legitimacy, albeit starting from a false premise, it provided an alternate definition for human identity than what was found in the Bible.

---

5. Descartes, *Discourse*, I.14.
6. Descartes, *Discourse*, IV.1.

Part I: Joy and Its Loss

For many generations, the total fragmentation of identity in Western society was held off by the strong lingering threads of biblical authority. Even if a person left everything he knew and lost all the ways he was known, wherever he went he would find others conversant with the Bible and accepting its authority (whether or not it was followed). In society more broadly, even through the mid-twentieth century, the moral framework derived from the Bible was held to be best for people and was assumed as the foundation of Law. The very project of the Enlightenment from Descartes onward, to provide morality based on Reason rather than biblical revelation, still assumed the same virtues and moral norms of the Christian tradition. The attempt was to arrive at Christian virtues without religion. But even that Enlightenment project failed.

It was the dissolving of this moral framework and agreement about social norms that inspired W.B. Yeats in his poem, "The Second Coming":

> Turning and turning in the widening gyre
> The falcon cannot hear the falconer;
> Things fall apart; the centre cannot hold;
> Mere anarchy is loosed upon the world,
> The blood-dimmed tide is loosed, and everywhere
> The ceremony of innocence is drowned;

Written in 1919, the poem registers the shock at the horrible devastation of World War I and the unbounded willingness to use every scientific advancement in order to kill and destroy. People began to realize that without common values and morality, without common Christianity, and without a shared past, nothing would restrain men in the will to dominate. In such a state, "Things fall apart; the centre cannot hold; / Mere anarchy is loosed upon the world." Without such a center, other solutions tried to provide ultimate answers to identity and meaning, loosing their "blood-dimmed tide" as Yeats foresaw. Fascism and Communism may have been the bloodiest, but they have not been the only efforts to replace Christianity.

By the end of the twentieth century, the West saw the end of traditional forms of authority having a dominant cultural influence, even in the naturally conservative legal and medical fields. The shift from objective definitions received from the past has been displaced by subjective, personal judgment. In Western society, since "What is good?" is no longer connected to what God had revealed in the Bible, what church and family had communicated, and what the laws had enshrined, then anything might be good. Without an appeal either to inherited customs or to objective truth about the meaning of humans and accountability to God, the individual has become the one who will decide who he or she is and what is good. Along with standards of right and wrong, identity has become a matter of personal creativity.

What does this shift in identity and morality mean for seeking joy? It means that modern societies have intensified certain forms of suffering having to do with a human being's relationship to the self, others, and creation. It means that joy is being sought in isolation, in places and by means where it cannot be found. It means that the Fall continues to work out its consequences on the large scale as well as the small. But when we consider these changes historically and recognize alternatives, many that are still present in pre-modern societies, we can also discover that God has left us wisdom to help us in our time of need. He has left us his Word that reveals his ways, and he has given us heavenly wisdom to consider and prophesy in our times rather than be passive recipients of corrupt cultural norms.

Christian leaders across the global south would do well to heed the example of what has happened in the West. Even now, cities in developing countries across the world are swelling with young people who have left their villages looking for economic and social opportunities. In most cases they will be severely disappointed. In all cases, they will be profoundly separated from traditional society. Moreover, society as a whole is being ruptured just as it was in the West. The rise of individualism brings with it the destruction of custom and traditional ways of seeing the world. Over the last few years, I (Cedric) have frequently debated with Western-educated atheist apologists on radio and TV as they argue for the total secularization of Rwandan society. As happened in the West, their desire is to see African culture lose its sense of the spiritual. But as I argue regularly, it is not yet too late to proactively shape society by preserving the wisdom of tradition through the lens of the Bible. Even in the teeming cities, churches can be the most significant link to the values of village life and can provide a surrogate family from the one that has been left behind in the countryside. Amidst emerging individualism, the church can provide a place for the newly autonomous man or woman, but within the love, support, and accountability of a family.

The common isolation and despair of modern city life does not have to be our experience. Whether in the country or the city, life in the kingdom of God reconnects us to the design for which God created us. Through his Spirit empowering us for life in community, we can begin to taste again the meaningful life, contentment, and peace given in the Garden. We can taste joy.

In Part II of this book, we will examine paths to joy and common hindrances that need not be the completely debilitating experience they often become. Although much of our focus is on Western society, where the examples are full grown, the Global South is not far behind. Especially where technology is spreading a story of individualism, modernity is bringing its special forms of suffering and fragmentation. To these experiences, we will apply insights from God's Word that can help shift perspective from perceiving the suffering according to a paradigm of death to perceiving according to the wisdom of God's kingdom and everlasting life.

It is our contention that when perception aligns with God's kingdom, joy is the result. The objective circumstances might not change, but when a suffering Christian begins to perceive life in fellowship with the Holy Spirit, in connection with other believers, and in trusting obedience to God, then he will find himself within God's design. In this wisdom of God, he will have access to the peace of God. He will find joy.

Getting Up to Speed: The Poverty of Modernity

QUESTIONS FOR REFLECTION

What is most appealing to you about premodern life as described in the chapter?

In the shift to modernity and an individualistic outlook, what feels like the greatest gain and the worst loss?

Since Christians are not to follow the norms of our society in an unthinking way, what are some ways that Christians can organize our lives to resist some of the isolating tendencies of modernity? What can you change in your life?

PART II

Paths to Rediscovering Joy

4

The Joy of Knowing God

THE RESTORATION OF JOY in human life blossoms from restored knowledge of the Almighty God. He is the Alpha and Omega, the first and the last, so all right things begin in him. Every person's story finds meaning within the life and story of what God has done. But as we explored in chapter 2, without true knowledge of God, we are left to our own broken resources. For any person to have joy, God must reveal himself. And it turns out that he wants to!

This restorative power of God's revelation comes through clearly in the book *Bruchko*, Bruce Olson's autobiographical account of bringing the news of Jesus Christ to the Motilone tribe of Venezuela. Olson tells of patiently living as a member of the completely isolated jungle people, waiting for the Lord to open a channel of meaningful connection between their culture's view of life and the Lord Jesus. After four years of learning the Motilone language and entering deep friendship with a young man named Bobarishora (Bobby), Olson had yet to find a bridge to communicate the gift of eternal life. As he walked with Bobby in the jungle, he came upon two men who were in an agony from the death of a friend and were digging a hole to try to find God, who had left them long ago. It was his first introduction to the way the Motilone thought about death, and the utter hopelessness of their story. In

Part II: Paths to Rediscovering Joy

that moment, Olson told a parable that illustrated the movement of God towards humans in Jesus Christ. The parable connected with Bobby, and the Holy Spirit came to him and began to give him understanding.[1]

When Bobby felt it was time to share his discovery with his people, he used their favorite medium of sharing significant news: singing. From a hammock slung fifty feet high in the tribal lodge, Bobby began to sing the knowledge that had come to him. For hour upon hour, he sang the story of the Motilone people, legend upon legend, leading to the coming of Jesus among men. As he sang, the Motilone stories took on new meaning as the truth of their Creator was woven into them. Through Bobby's song, the Word—the knowledge and truth of God—flowed again into this people's identity. More and more of the tribe took up the song as their own. The result was overflowing joy. In a short time, almost the entire tribe had entrusted their lives to Jesus Christ.

The transformation of the Motilone illustrates what happens when the revealed knowledge of God does its designed work. As discussed in chapter 2, when people turned from the Wisdom and Word of God and embraced Satan's corrupt version of the world, wrong understanding of everything worked its way into the most basic human assumptions and impulses. The Word of God had spoken people into existence, and without the Word's indwelling, each and every person has been born into corruption, confusion, and the unraveling of existence. Without hope of eternal life, without the power to sustain goodness, people everywhere have sought to stem the outworking of death for as long as possible. But then "the Word became flesh and dwelt among us, full of grace and truth" (John 1:14).

Jesus Christ brought the Word and Wisdom of God back to human nature, surpassing the knowledge of the first Adam by bringing to man the supreme dignity of God himself. Where the first Adam had a soul that bore the image of God, Jesus brought God himself into Man. Joining the nature of Man and the nature of God, Jesus reunited forever what had been severed at the Fall.

1. Olson, *Bruchko*, 122-28.

Resurrecting his human body in his triumph over death, Jesus brought restored humanity into the Trinity. In this move of everlasting significance, Jesus accomplished what had been planned for Man from before creation: a perfected human nature having complete knowledge of God.

As the risen Lord Jesus rejoined the Father, God sent the Holy Spirit into the world to awaken and dwell with everyone who calls on his name, repents, and submits to him (Acts 2:33, 38). Those who receive the Holy Spirit experience the restoration of God's life-giving Word to a nature that was dead in sin. We know, of course, that our flesh continues to suffer the consequences of the fallen creation, but the inner man is made alive by the Holy Spirit. Even before his Cross, Jesus taught the disciples what the indwelling of the Spirit would mean for them. He promised that the Spirit "will teach you all things and bring to your remembrance all that I have said to you" (John 14:26), and "When the Spirit of truth comes, he will guide you into all the truth" (John 16:13). The Holy Spirit brings the Word to enlighten human understanding and correct the false visions of God that we imagine for ourselves. Through the Spirit, the Bible reveals God to us and guides us to see God as he is, not as we might wish him to be.

RELATIONSHIP RESTORED: THE JOY OF ADOPTION

As Jesus taught his disciples about the coming Holy Spirit by which he and the Father would dwell in them, he built upon his continual teaching about the kind of relationship that he had come to restore. God had chosen a nation, and in that choosing had indicated what he would later do. He was moving to adopt individuals to be members of his everlasting spiritual family. He would be their Father, they his children.

In the prayer Jesus gave to his disciples, "The Lord's Prayer," he instructed them to address God as "Father." Then he gave them an illustration in which he assured them the heavenly Father desires to give good gifts—even the best gift of himself—to those who ask him (Luke 11:1–13). If weak and corrupt earthly fathers don't play the trickster with their children when asked for good things, then surely they could trust the perfect God to act in their best interest. Jesus wanted them to understand that as they become disciples of God and give their lives to know and love him, not only will he guide them in his ways but he will do so as a Father. The indwelling of God's Spirit would seal this everlasting relationship. What a glorious truth! The God who made and rules the universe knows each of his creatures personally and intimately. When we yield to him, he adopts us as his beloved children.

By this adoption, which Jesus explained at length in his last discourse recorded in John (chapters 13–17), believers in Jesus experience the restoration of God's design for humans: increasing knowledge of God within the security of being completely known. The more we inwardly digest the words of Scripture and the indwelling Word makes them part of our thinking, the more we realize God knows us in our weakness but loves us nonetheless. On every page of the Bible we find our own frailty displayed: the inconstancies of the patriarchs, the idolatries and viciousness of Israel, the kings in their selfishness and folly, and even the disciples in their pettiness and obstinance. And right alongside we find the faithfulness of God, his long-suffering and abounding steadfast love.

To get a better hold of the joy of adoption, consider God's call of Abram the Chaldean. In this call, the Lord says, "Go from your country and your kindred and your father's house to the land that I will show you" (Gen 12:1). God knows what will be hard for Abram, and he shapes his call around the core identity markers for this man of the ancient world. His call narrows in on Abram's sense of himself: country, kindred, nuclear family. Each term moves more and more fundamental to Abram's identity. Ancient identity was inseparable from family and clan. Modern Western readers tend to feel alienated from the constant reference to family in Scriptures, to the *-ites* that appear everywhere. Amalekites, Amorites, Hittites, Israelites, Danites, Jebusites, etc., along with those overwhelming genealogies. While they feel distant from us, those markers are in the text because they were core to the identity of those being discussed. Abram, his family, and everyone he had known were worshippers of the Babylonian pantheon of gods; Ur and Haran, the places Abram had lived, were devoted to the moon-god. Their lives were embedded in every pattern of life in Chaldea. So when God calls Abram to leave his country, kindred, and family, he is calling him to leave his entire identity behind.

But consider God's gentleness in this call. Even as he calls Abram to lose his identity, he offers one in its place. In parallel to what Abram will lose, the Lord says, "I will make of you a nation, I will bless you, I will make your name great. I will bless those who bless you, and him who dishonors you I will curse, and in you all the families of the earth shall be blessed'" (Gen 12:2–3). It is easy for us to miss the magnitude of these words. Yes, Abram will lose country, kin, and family—he will lose all that identifies him and makes sense of his life. But he will be given a *new identity bound up with the Lord himself*. He will become a family and a nation with a new name and a new heritage which is tied inextricably to God. The Lord identifies *himself* with Abram—his family with Abram's: "I will bless those who bless you, and him who dishonors you I will curse." Behavior toward Abram will be treated as behavior toward God. They are the same family, with God as Father. And in this family, "all the families of the earth shall be blessed." So even as God invites Abram to renounce his life, God also lays out a new life, a new identity, and a new story.

In Romans, Paul says those of us who claim Christ as Lord have made the same declaration that Abraham did and so have become part of his family heritage: "he is the father of all who believe by faith" (Rom 4:16). Like him, we have made the great renunciation. We have transferred the core of our identity into Christ. This Abram-turned-Abraham is thus archetypal for all those who are of his family of faith. Receiving God as sovereign and accepting his words as right and true, we begin to know him as he is. Becoming children of his own family, we come to learn that our lives, each one, matter to our Father and have ultimate significance. More and more we find that we are known, and to our great joy we find

Part II: Paths to Rediscovering Joy

that God loves us still. Despite our wavering, our doubts, and our faithlessness, he remains faithful to us and committed to our place in his plans. Like Abraham, the new identity means we are part of God's plans for rescuing and reshaping his world.

The joy of restoration to our designed identity as children of God empowers Christians to endure the loss of other identity markers. I (Ben) will never forget the first time I got a glimpse into this truth. When I was a child of eight or nine years old, a Nigerian man was baptized in our church. He had come to study at the University of Tennessee, near where I grew up, and through friendship with a Christian had come to know Jesus as Lord and savior. But he was a Muslim. To accept baptism would publicly and irreversibly shift his identity. Giving testimony prior to his baptism, he told that he would soon return to his home village and declare his faith in Jesus, and his father would be honor-bound to kill him. Choking through tears, he expressed that it was his love for his family, and his desire that they too would know Jesus, that compelled him to return. Along with this courageous love, what stunned me as a child was the way he burst from the water—like an explosion—and then gripped the sides of the baptismal pool in order to fix his eyes on the congregation, his new family of faith. The joy from his face radiated. In what little way I could, I understood that I was seeing the power and the secure confidence to face anything, even death. Death was no longer the ultimate reality. It had been replaced by everlasting life with a loving Father. This new identity gave joy.

I (Cedric) found a similar inexpressible joy when God revealed himself to me. This movement from Islam to knowing God as Father not only gave me a place in the everlasting family of faith, but I also found healing as a son of my human father.[2] Claiming his Islamic right to reject his wife for any reason, my father had abandoned our family after the 1994 Rwandan Genocide and left my mother, siblings, and me to struggle for survival. From nine years old, I grew up hating him, even plotting to murder him.

---

2. The full story of Cedric's conversion is told in *Dying in Islam, Rising in Christ*.

When Jesus revealed himself to me and saved my life, my father added to my pains by trying to kill me through poisoning and arranging assassination. As a Muslim sheikh, he was honor-bound to kill a child who converted away from Islam. At each attempt on my life, the Holy Spirit unmasked the danger or steered me away from it, but the pain of my own father's attempted murders weighed heavily on me.

When I was baptized, something powerful happened in my heart. A helpful pastor explained that the early church understood baptism as the adoption ceremony for new believers entering the family of God, and that it was common for them to take on a new name in token of their new identity, similar to Abram becoming Abraham and Jacob becoming Israel when they met their heavenly Father. This seemed right for me as I had moved from following Allah to knowing God as Father, and I left the identity of Swidiq and became Cedric (the name of a Christian I had known as a child). Through that baptism I received not only assurance of my adoption by God but also grace for my earthly father. Knowing I was loved, I was enabled to love one who wanted me dead. God helped me see that my dad's violence towards me was really flowing from his own fears of shame and death. Where there had been only a gaping wound, I found compassion. As I pursued relationship with my father, my heavenly Father filled me with joy at the great privilege of showing his own mercy and love. Not only did I have the joy that God knows me, but I had come to know him enough that I could tell others how wonderful he is. The more I told of him, the more I was filled with laughter. I got to show my dad what my new family was like, and it was unmistakably different than anything he had ever seen. In time, he too wanted the peace and joy that I had found, a joy that marked my new family.

JOY FROM SURRENDER TO THE WORD

Having the restored identity as children of God means there is a family resemblance, a salvation to be worked out with fear and trembling (Phil 2:12–13). Jesus taught his disciples that the Holy

Spirit—the indwelling Word—would work with the words God had already spoken, both through his prophets in the Old Testament and through the very words he gave the apostles. As Paul wrote, "All Scripture is breathed out by God and profitable for teaching, for reproof, for correction, and for training in righteousness, that the man of God may be complete, equipped for every good work" (2 Tim 3:16–17). The indwelling Spirit would take God's Word breathed out and received into the heart of Man, so that the Word would be "living and active" in the inner person. When God's Spirit gives a person understanding of God's words, the primary function is restoring the lost knowledge of the Almighty God, the personal and relational knowledge of a soul with its maker. The person who allows God's Spirit to use God's words to challenge, correct, and cleanse him will find the life-giving Word of God transforming every aspect of his interior life.

Cooperating with the enlivening work of God's Word is what Paul urges on the church at Rome. He writes, "I appeal to you therefore, brothers, by the mercies of God, to present your bodies as a living sacrifice, holy and acceptable to God, which is your spiritual worship. Do not be conformed to this world, but be transformed by the renewal of your mind, that by testing you may discern what is the will of God, what is good and acceptable and perfect" (Rom 12:1–2). The recipe is remarkable in its simplicity. A human being living in the physical world has to bring the whole self to God. We cannot actually bring only our minds while leaving our bodies behind. We can't send our minds to church while our bodies stay at home watching a football game. But when we bring ourselves and allow the Lord's Word to teach us, we find that he himself does the work of transformation and renewal, changing our affections and desires as we yield our hearts to his Word.

There is no shortcut to surrendering our minds to the Word. Not long after I (Cedric) had left Islam to follow Christ, the Lord Jesus was very gracious to give me several dramatic experiences to reshape my heart for him. I had been reborn into his kingdom, but I was like someone who had newly immigrated to a foreign country; I needed to learn the ways of my adoptive land. On one

The Joy of Knowing God

occasion, as I was sitting wide awake in my room, I had a vision of Jesus entering the room and moving towards me.[3] As he walked forward, peace came before him and calmed my terrified mind. Strangely, he was holding a toothbrush. I was frozen as he approached me and stuck the toothbrush in my mouth, then disappeared. Instantly, I was speaking with joy and exhilaration in a language I did not know. As one who had been a vocal apologist for Islam, often blaspheming Jesus, my mouth had been full of corruption. Since then, I have been deeply thankful for this vision because it assured me that he had cleansed my mouth for his work. While several other visions dealt with other facets of my life being restored, none of these visionary experiences could provide the true story of God and our place in it. They gave assurance, they corrected misunderstanding, and they revealed God's character, but only the written Word could bring the transformative knowledge to guide my thinking.

As a Muslim imam, I had memorized the Quran. How much more did I need the Word of God! Most importantly, I had learned that God is alive and speaking, so I needed to be able to hear and discern what the true voice of the Holy Spirit sounds like. Where better to learn his voice than from his written Word? Alongside hearing truly, I also needed to think rightly about God. I poured over the Bible, asking God to teach me about him and correct the ways of thinking I had received from Islam. With single-minded devotion to learn about God, I found myself and my whole conception of the world being re-written. The terrible rebellion of all mankind was clear; the inevitable necessity of punishment and wrath was unavoidable; God's prepared path for redemption stood out large in this history of Israel; the divergent paths and resistance of the nations were laid bare; and the passionate love of God for his world shone bright in Jesus. As I absorbed the Bible, the Lord re-wrote my understanding of the world, the ways of God with man, and salvation according to his people's inspired history rather than according to Islamic tradition.

---

3. We recount the full context of this vision and the background to it in *Dying*, chapters 15–16.

Part II: Paths to Rediscovering Joy

Likewise, the Bible gave me a vocabulary for talking about my own experience of salvation and the amazing joy I was discovering. With the Scriptures more and more filling my mind and giving patterns to my thought, I came to rely more and more on the Lord to bring a phrase or passage to mind when I needed wisdom or insight. I learned that trusting the Lord to give understanding of my moments was a sure path to joy.

This may sound too passive, especially for the action-oriented, do-it-yourself American, but the gospel of our salvation is implied even here. We have never been able to save ourselves, cleanse ourselves, or pull our souls up by our soul-bootstraps. Spiritual work is done spiritually, and the author of our salvation must continue to be the one who works in our spiritual inner lives. As we are reminded in Ephesians, "when you heard the word of truth, the gospel of your salvation, and believed in him, [you] were sealed with the promised Holy Spirit." Notice that the believer's work is to believe, while the saving and the sealing belong to God. And that same word of truth continues to work for the transformation of our lives. For that reason, Paul follows quickly with the prayer "that the God of our Lord Jesus Christ, the Father of glory, may give you the Spirit of wisdom and of revelation in the knowledge of him, having the eyes of your hearts enlightened, that you may know what is the hope to which he has called you, what are the riches of his glorious inheritance in the saints, and what is the immeasurable greatness of his power toward us who believe" (Eph 1:13–19). When God's redeemed people yield to the Holy Spirit working in their lives, applying the living Word in a myriad of particular ways, God's people come to know him again. And according to our design, having the Word brings us again into the path of discovering God for which we were made in Paradise. As the Westminster Catechism rightly grasps, "Man's chief end is to glorify God and enjoy him forever." This glorification and enjoyment begin with the restoration of God's Word in a person.

As both the Romans and Ephesians passages suggest, being transformed by the renewal of our minds and having our hearts enlightened happens as we come to know God more. This is what we were made for. Like Adam and Eve walking with God in the Garden, where each day was richer than the last and brought more understanding of God and his world, so a new world is opened up for a Christian. By restoring his Word to our souls, we can re-enter the true human quest to know and delight in our Creator. We have been promised that God's own breathed-out words of the Bible will reveal him. We note his consistent character in his interactions with Israel in the Old Testament; we see his nature and perfection shown in his Law; we heed his own self-description; and principally in Jesus we come to appreciate what God is like. The Bible shows us God. But something more than merely intellectual happens when we spend time in the presence of God, letting his Spirit apply his words. Just as God gave increasing knowledge to Adam and Eve as they came to know him experientially, so restored humans come to know God intimately when his Spirit causes his Word to grow us in his character and true wisdom.

My (Ben's) sister has shown me this process well. Her son was born with a rare genetic disorder, which at the time of his diagnosis was considered fatal by the age of 15. At one year old, my nephew underwent a stem-cell transplant using umbilical cord cells from a healthy child, and he spent over a hundred days in a hospital and months more at the Ronald McDonald House. As my sister sat with him day after day, for long stretches unable to touch him and daily wondering if he would survive, her heart hardened to God. Her husband found encouragement in the promises of God, but she felt tricked and toyed with. She knew God had the power to heal her son in an instant, but he withheld that gift. She began to imagine him as a hard and cold God.

But the transplant worked. My nephew began to produce life-giving blood rather than protein-deficient, life-destroying blood. Although his body began to heal, and many corrective surgeries awaited him, my sister's heart had become dry and hard. As they went through surgery after surgery, each time she feared God would now choose to take her son. For a few years, she couldn't pray and couldn't bear Christians talking about how kind and merciful God had been. They went to church, but it was embittering to see so many healthy children and the ignorant bliss with which their parents took that health for granted. Nevertheless, as she says, "Fortunately, I did still desire fellowship with believers, like a wallflower who wants to go to the dance, even if she never plans to join in," so she joined a Community Bible Study group. It was here that the Word did its work.

There was no profound moment, no piercing light into the dungeon of despair; just the slow and growing light of truth. Through months and years of coming to his Word, the Holy Spirit changed her view of God. As she tells it, "Trust in God comes from knowing God, and knowing him only comes from seeking him in his Word. I came to know him more and more, and I found that he was trustworthy." Without fanfare, she realized one day that her understanding of God had diametrically changed from the terrifying God of death to the gentle God who stands with us in deep and abiding love. In contrast to the instantaneous change that most of us wish for, she found that as she came to his Word regularly, God showed himself to her bit by bit, week by week, surgery by surgery. Her joy unfolded as a morning glory opens its bloom with the dawn.

If the originating source of joy is knowing God, then we grow in the capacity for joy as we come to know him more and more. As my sister found, like others in this chapter, discovering the true nature of God not only liberated her from the terrors of my nephew's death and from the misery of isolated despair, it also changed her perception of everything. The good God wanted her to see in the way that he sees, but first, she had to look at him in order for her spiritual eyes to have everything else in proper perspective and proportion. The uncompromising truth is that he is the center of all, but just as essential as his sovereignty is his character: the Great I Am is who he is, not as each of us imagines him when left to ourselves. He is who he is, and he is good. Because of our fall, we cannot arrive at the true nature of God on our own. He had to come in Jesus Christ to reveal himself, to save us, and to give us back our capacity to know him rightly and truly.

It is God's part to reveal himself, to let himself be known in each tiny facet of his infinite being. It is our part to seek him, to avail ourselves to what he will reveal. To the extent that we yield time and attention to his speaking Word, we willingly cooperate with his intention to be known. We have the promise of Jesus himself that this desire will be granted: "Ask, and it will be given to you; seek, and you will find; knock, and it will be opened to you. For everyone who asks receives, and the one who seeks finds, and to the one who knocks it will be opened. What father among you, if his son asks for a fish, will instead of a fish give him a serpent; or if he asks for an egg, will give him a scorpion? If you then, who are evil, know how to give good gifts to your children, how much more will the heavenly Father give the Holy Spirit to those who ask him!" (Luke 11:9–13).

QUESTIONS FOR REFLECTION

Like Abraham found, becoming adopted by God sometimes means letting go of other identity markers you've shaped your life around. Are there any parts of an old identity that you are clinging to but that you know God is replacing with himself?

God's Word often feels out of step with our society? Are there messages from American society that you hold as having higher authority in your life than God's Word?

Sometimes our fears or expectations cloud our trust of God. Are there certain fears or disappointed hopes that cause you to keep God at arm's length? What truth about God's character applies to those fears?

/ 5

The Joy of Living God's Ways

When God began his plan of restoration by creating a family of faith, his word was given directly to Abraham, Isaac, and Jacob so that accepting his Word meant believing promises made directly to them. But have you ever noticed that Abraham, Isaac, and Jacob didn't even know how to worship God? Their faith was expressed through believing his promises and showing trust, through obedience, whenever he spoke to them. They were a family of faith, but they were not *formed* as a people living according to their Father's ways. They were God's family but did not yet resemble their Father.

The books of Moses do not tell us how the Hebrews worshiped God while they were living as slaves in Egypt. Certainly they kept and told the stories of their fathers Abraham, Isaac, Jacob, and Joseph. They kept circumcision as a distinct marker. They knew they were not Egyptians and so did not worship Egyptian gods, nor would they have been allowed to by their masters. The Egyptians made sure that Hebrews knew they were slaves. Servitude was their identity and their meaning; it was their purpose; it shaped every day; it crushed every hope; it was their story. No doubt they struggled to remember God's promises to their fathers and to believe them.

The Joy of Living God's Ways

When God delivered this nation of broken people, defined by lies and hopelessness, he had a major reconstructive operation to do. They did not even know his proper name, and he came to them as not only the Creator God but their own loving Father and King. After breaking them out of prison, he brought them to Mt. Sinai. At that point it was time for them to take on the family resemblance, for their heavenly Father's character to shape his family's character. In Exodus 19:6, he says, "Although the whole earth is mine, you will be for me a kingdom of priests and a holy nation." Immediately, then, he gives them the Law of the Covenant.

Unlike the laws of the nations that tried to deal with hostile, capricious gods while making society workable, the Lord unveiled what would be for their good according to how he had made them. The difference was obvious. Recounting the giving of the Law at Sinai, Moses says, "See, I have taught you decrees and laws as the Lord my God commanded. Observe them carefully, for this will show your wisdom and understanding to the nations, who will say, 'Surely this great nation is a wise and understanding people.' What other nation is so great as to have their gods near them the way the Lord our God is near us? And what other nation is so great as to have such righteous decrees and laws as this body of laws I am setting before you today?" (Deut. 4:5-6). They were aware God was doing something very different with them than the kind of relationship other nations had with their gods.

For starters, God taught them that his Law, communicating his ways, was given for their *good*. Because he perfectly understood human design, as well as all the horrid tendencies into which fallen humans always slide, he was providing the best possible norms and practices that would turn their attentions, energies, and affections to what would enable them to prosper. By regulating offerings of animals and crops, the Law taught them not to set their hearts and hopes on material things, but to trust in the God who owns all things. By setting rhythms of work and rest, the Law restrained Israel from depending on their own continuous and futile efforts to shape their future. They were taught to stop their work in order to honor and celebrate the God from whom all good things flow.

Part II: Paths to Rediscovering Joy

And in the midst of that rest and worship, with God exalted in their midst, they would find themselves in proper relationship to one another. Thus, the Law would help them to be *holy* because he is holy. His Law was not just about society being livable and restraining people from destroying each other; his Law was to conform them to holiness, to goodness, so that they could live well with each other and with their Creator.

Inseparably, his Law allowed for the nearness and personal presence of the holy God by dealing with the obstacle of human sin (at least in a temporary way before his own sacrifice could deal with it once for all). By following the cycle of yearly sacrifice, Israel's sin was atoned for and their sin sent away. Essentially, the Law provided a means by which a major step could be taken to restore the identity that was lost at the Fall. The Almighty God was again near people—he was walking with them in a pillar of cloud and fire, meeting with them in a tent—and his Word was being given to them. This is what made them the People of God, living in covenant with God. So how did it work?

Sometimes we read back our life with God into the Old Testament. We forget that they were not given the Holy Spirit to indwell them. In the Old Covenant, God shaped his people from the outside, in. Like Paul explains, the Law was like a teacher, constraining passions and directing desires (Gal 3:24–25). In teaching the people what was sinful and hostile to God, the Law was meant to internalize God's ways. A person with faith believed what God had taught and followed the Law out of love for him, and the net result was a life shaped in a way that pleased the Holy One and was also good for them. They were conformed from the outside, in, like a mold pressed on soft clay. Their deliverance from four hundred years of slavery in Egypt had rendered them soft clay again. The covenant with God was to leave the impression of an image on that clay. It was the image of God. Through that covenant, God was teaching about the restoration of his design in human beings. It depicted all the blessings associated with the original Edenic design, including a resulting sense of joy.

The Joy of Living God's Ways

Although this covenant was a teacher, it was not sufficient to bring about what it taught. As Hebrews says, "the law has but a shadow of the good things to come instead of the true form of these realities, it can never, by the same sacrifices that are continually offered every year, make perfect those who draw near... for it is impossible for the blood of bulls and goats to take away sin" (Heb 10:1). The Law, though good, did not restore their souls but only taught about restoration. It showed the difference of God's ways and the ways of the nations. In other words, Israel still had to contend with the basic way a human works. Summarizing the sixteenth century Thomas Cranmer's understanding of the principle, Canon Ashley Null says, "What the heart loves, the will chooses, and the mind justifies. The mind doesn't direct the will. The mind is actually captive to what the will wants, and the will itself, in turn, is captive to what the heart wants."[1] Even by conforming the nation and at best internalizing God's ways in the conscience, the Law could not touch the fountainhead of the heart.

From the time of Adam and Eve's rejection of God's life in them, God's aim was to recreate humanity so that his design would be restored, in which his personal Word—his own Life—would be inseparable from an awakened person. The Law could shape desire and behavior, but it could not bring God's image back to the heart of Man. Something else was in store. In Ezekiel 36, God says,

> "For I will take you out of the nations; I will gather you from all the countries. I will sprinkle clean water on you, and you will be clean; I will cleanse you from all your impurities and from all your idols. I will give you a new heart and put a new spirit in you; I will remove from you your heart of stone and give you a heart of flesh. And I will put my Spirit in you and move you to follow my decrees and be careful to keep my laws." (36:24–27)

This is our Covenant, the New Covenant in the Spirit. Again, God himself had to establish it, which he did through his death and resurrection, satisfying the requirements of the Old Covenant. He sprinkles clean. He cleanses from impurities and from idolatry.

1. Null, "On Cranmer."

Part II: Paths to Rediscovering Joy

He gives a new heart. But notice that *God's ways do not go away*; they are part of this renewal. He says, "I will put my Spirit in you and move you to follow my decrees and be careful to keep my laws." Concerning the Spirit, Jesus says, "the Counselor, the Holy Spirit, whom the Father will send in my name, will teach you all things and will remind you of everything I have said to you" (John 14:26). So there is still a law for the Spirit to teach, and desires towards which one must be moved. As with God's Law given at Mt. Sinai, it is not just making life livable; rather it is about living well, living into our design, living in harmony with our God, so that his image is restored in us. So how does this indwelling Law shape our identity as God's People, and how does it bring a sense of joy?

First, instead of working from the outside, in, the Holy Spirit brings the ways of God into the heart of a person so that his Law works from the inside, out. The Old Law worked to shape obedience and train desire through performance and the rhythms of life. As a gift to the temporal world, that is good and helpful for all. The Jewish-Christian tradition has brought precious principles into the world, such as the inherent dignity of every person, impartial justice for people of all social classes, as well as recognizing the essentially destructive nature of disrespecting parents, killing, lying, stealing, adultery (along with loose sexual mores generally), and jealousy. Every society needs the gift of their Creator's wisdom for establishing the best ways for people to live together. But the Law of the Spirit corrects the normal process of how God's ways conform individuals and the people of God.

As we considered in the previous chapter, the Gospel message acknowledges the desperation and failure of perfectability when attempted by strength of will. We cannot change our hearts and live God's ways simply by conformity: by our actions or by wanting. God must do it. The Spirit who fills our hearts must work change in our desires, deep in the inner person. The Spirit directs our desires to things that please God. In other words, the Spirit brings the Law into our hearts and directs our mind to follow suit. Rather than conforming our behavior like the Old Covenant, the Spirit transforms our minds, giving us a new heart and a new identity. From a transformed heart, a new way of walking will emerge.

COOPERATING WITH LOVE: WALKING IN THE LIGHT

Some of my (Ben's) in-laws have a very distinct walk. My wife's brother and sister walk exactly like their dad. A couple times, from a distance I have recognized that I am seeing one of them but not sure which until they get close enough to see some features. We can all think of remarkable family resemblances—not just how we look but how a family uses their hands when talking, or tones, or posture, but also ways of handling conflict or expressing excitement, habits, even recognizable family ambitions, aims, and desires. We know that families pass along genetic code, which only enhances the imitative potential for kids. People have always seen that children learn by imitation. The glaring result of this combination of nature and nurture is family resemblance—the ways of a family and a people.

As we have been examining, Christians have something like a new genetic code. Like Abraham discussed above, we have the story of God's People into which we have been drawn. More significantly, we have undergone an essential transfer, which the Bible expresses in several ways: we were *adopted* out of Adam's fallen family into the Redeemed Family of God, and we were *reborn*, becoming new creations connected to Christ by his Spirit. Our belonging in this family is set down by an unbreakable Covenant guaranteed by the blood of Jesus and the indwelling Holy Spirit.

Flowing from this reality of new birth in the everlasting family and a new heart by the Spirit, it is now for us to consider the family resemblance. Second Corinthians 3:14 says, "We, who with unveiled faces all reflect the Lord's glory, are being transformed into his likeness with ever-increasing glory, which comes from the Lord, who is the Spirit." One might then reasonably ask, what of our Father God is being shaped in us as his Holy Spirit restores and transforms us increasingly into the image of God? Likewise, how do we willingly cooperate so that the joy of the Lord becomes more of a norm for us?

To the Ephesian church working out this same subject of living out their new identity, Paul wrote, "Be imitators of God as dearly loved children and walk in love, just as Christ loved us and gave himself up for us as a fragrant offering and sacrifice to God" (5:1–2). It is a command that assumes the restored identity that we have been discussing: be imitators of God *as dearly loved children*. There is the new reality. We his people are most essentially his dearly loved children. Even while the command is being given, the basis of it is actually the most prominent aspect to it: the love of God. The Creator God is a loving God, and he loves people. In one sentence, a form of the word *agape* is used three times. We are beloved children, and we know we are dearly loved because Christ loved us and gave himself up to death for us.

The command is remarkable in its simplicity: live (or walk) as who you actually are. Imitate your eternal Father whose Spirit is now in you. You have imitated your earthly parents and you have lived according to your physical genes; now embrace your redeemed identity as God's boy or God's girl and imitate him. Do not resist the family resemblance, but embrace it. Lest there be confusion about the primary family trait, Paul spells it out: "walk in love (or live a life of love) just as Christ loved us and gave himself up for us as a fragrant offering and sacrifice to God."

Considering, then, the restoration of human hearts in accordance with the Life of God, the primary trait of God's family is *agape*. This essential posture of heart is the love that was most noticeably lost at the Fall because it is connected to God's Spirit. This love is not in the bones and blood; it is not in our instincts looking out for our survival or our own good; instead, it is of the Spirit of God. Even the Greeks, who used the word originally, thought it was the love of the gods alone, unless they imparted it to a human. In *The Four Loves*, C.S. Lewis calls it "divine gift-love," and he explains that *agape* is the character of God himself, which "desires what is simply best for the beloved" and loves "what is not naturally lovable."[2]

Earlier in Ephesians Paul had said as much. "Though we were dead in our trespasses and sins, following the prince of the power of the air, gratifying the cravings of our sinful nature and following its desires and thoughts... nevertheless because of his great love for us, God who is rich in mercy made us alive with Christ" (Eph. 2:1–5). He loved what was unlovable in order to bring about our good. He suffered and did what had to be done for those he loved. As John says, "This is how we know what love is: Jesus Christ laid down his life for us" (1 John 3:16). This divine gift-love does not affirm what is evil even in the most dearly beloved; it cannot love evil. God's love cannot delight in what destroys his beloved children. But he moves towards us despite it, and he draws near to us in our wickedness in order to cleanse it and heal us of it. The love of God is a self-sacrificial love. Jesus was willing to suffer for the unlovable so that we might live. He offered himself up.

This self-sacrificial divine gift-love is what we are commanded to imitate, and it is our family trait that is supposed to work its way from his Spirit in our hearts all the way through our being, determining how we walk, both individually and collectively. It sounds like a high and impossible ideal. Were we to rely on our minds and wills, as those of the Old Covenant trying to keep the Law, it would certainly be beyond us. We have to accept that it is not in our flesh and blood to love like this. Divine gift-love must come from God's Spirit. Of course, God knows our weakness and the struggle of our infancy in a restored nature, so he gives us direction for our part.

In the sentences following the command to imitate God's love, he provides a key way for us to walk in self-sacrificial love. "At one time you were darkness, but now you are light in the Lord. Walk as children of light (for the fruit of light is found in all that is good and right and true), and try to discern what is pleasing to the Lord. Take no part in the unfruitful works of darkness, but instead expose them. For it is shameful even to speak of the things that they

---

2. Lewis, *Four Loves*, 164.

do in secret. But when anything is exposed by the light, it becomes visible, for anything that becomes visible is light." (Eph. 5:8–14). In other words, there must be a kind of sacrifice. The bringing of sin—described here as darkness—into the light is a form of sacrifice. Jesus personally brought us and our darkness into the light as he atoned for us. We follow our God and walk as children of light by making ongoing, living sacrifice of what remains dark in us. He says, "When anything is exposed by the light, it becomes visible, for anything that becomes visible is light."

The painful part of this move is that in a sacrifice something dies. We cannot expose our own darkness without some pain. To confess our sin out loud, to acknowledge that things we have done and thought are evil—are displeasing to God and are harmful to ourselves and others—is painful. Our pride dies a little. We lift our life to the Lord and say, "I know you have purchased my soul and set me free, now destroy these bits that won't live and don't belong with a redeemed life." Our self-protecting pride does not want that kind of raw exposure.

There is a fantastic depiction of this sacrifice in C.S. Lewis's *The Great Divorce*. Within Lewis's extended parable, there is a man who has come in proximity to the realm of heaven, but he has a horrible and animated lizard attached to him, which represents either a pattern of sin or a false identity. An angel approaches and offers to free the man by killing it. The miserable man begins negotiating, trying to put off the terrible necessity. He says, "I'd let you kill it now, but as a matter of fact I'm not feeling frightfully well today. It would be most silly to do it *now*. I'd need to be in good health for the operation. Some other day, perhaps." The angel replies, "There is no other day. All days are present now." The negotiation moves to a pitch:

"Get back! You're burning me. How can I tell you to kill it? You'd kill *me* if you did."

"It is not so."

"Why, you're hurting me now."

"I never said it wouldn't hurt you. I said it wouldn't kill you."

The Joy of Living God's Ways

"Oh, I know. You think I'm a coward. But it isn't that. Really it isn't. I say! Let me run back by tonight's bus and get an opinion from my own doctor. I'll come again the first moment I can."

"This moment contains all moments."

"Why are you torturing me? You are jeering at me. How *can* I let you tear me in pieces? If you wanted to help me, why didn't you kill the thing without asking me—before I knew? It would be all over by now if you had."

"I cannot kill it against your will. It is impossible. Have I your permission?"

The Angel's hands were almost closed on the Lizard, but not quite. Then the Lizard began chattering to the man so loud that even I could hear what it was saying.

What we come to understand as a lizard of bondage then bargains with him and promises all sorts of happiness and untold pleasures.

"Have I your permission?," said the Angel to the [man].

"I know it will kill me."

"It won't. But supposing it did?"

"You're right. It would be better to be dead than to live with this creature."

"Then I may?"

"Blast you! Go on, can't you? Get it over. Do what you like," bellowed the [man]: but ended, whimpering, "God help me, God help me."

Next moment the man gave a scream of agony such as I never heard on earth. The Burning One closed his bright grip on the reptile: twisted it, while it bit and writhed, and then flung it, broken-backed, on the turf.[3]

As Lewis's parable vividly shows in this encounter, a primary way we love God is by letting him love us, by cleansing us. By allowing his Spirit in us to correct our mis-ordered values and disordered desires, we are taking the step of being obedient. This is the life-giving obedience that Jesus describes, "If you love me, you will keep my commandments . . . . Whoever has my commandments

---

3. Lewis, *Great Divorce*, 109-10.

and keeps them, he it is who loves me. And he who loves me will be loved by my Father, and I will love him and manifest myself to him" (John 14:15, 21). The word "keep" might well be translated "treasure" or "hold fast," such that loving Jesus is expressed by clinging to and treasuring—valuing ultimately—the ways of God that he gives. But this offering of oneself to his reordering work will certainly not be painless. When his holiness meets our sin, the encounter inevitably changes us and generally leaves a mark. Think of Jacob who limped for the rest of his life after wrestling with God at Peniel.

But self-sacrificial love is the family trait of the newborn in Christ. The willingness to be transformed and to suffer for what is good flows from divine love alone, which has come to dwell in the adopted Christian. Self-sacrificial love, *agape*, is how we imitate Jesus, who offered up himself on behalf of all human sin. While he fully and truly died for our eternal salvation, we die to our pride so he can cleanse our character.

The fruit of this sacrifice is that we can love God for his own sake, without calculations for our self-interest, and can love others unselfishly. Paul says, "Walk as children of light (for the fruit of light is found in all that is good and right and true)" (Eph 5:8–9). Light, of course, is a symbol of God's own character: perfect goodness, purity, and righteousness. As we live in the light, we live and act according to what is good, worthwhile, right and true. As he says in Romans, "Be transformed by the renewing of your minds, that you may discern what is his good, pleasing, and perfect will" (Rom 12:2).

By walking in love and walking in light, we can participate in his self-giving love to others. Not only do we experience in ourselves the joy of self-sacrificial love, be we can pass it on to others. We can forgive others for their sins against us just as we have been forgiven by God. We can love what is not naturally or easily lovable, just as we have been loved by God in our wretchedness. By the operations of God's love in us, we can move towards what is unlovable, trusting that God will deal with the unlovable in others as he has done in us.

FROM BITTERNESS TO GRACE

Many people find that beginning to walk in love brings an unexpected gift. Christians who have harbored resentments or carried bitterness for many years are often surprised by a flood of joy upon giving up claims of the Law on those who have sinned against them. The joy is unexpected because the feeling of joy has been so long absent and so far from their reality that it has become inconceivable.

At some moment in the past, there was a betrayal by a family member or friend, or they themselves sinned in a way they could not (or would not) acknowledge. Unwilling or unable to bring the sin into the light, they nonetheless felt the moral pressure of the Law and its transgression, so they began rehearsing a story of the events, of the sin, and of those involved. And the story took root and hardened in their heart, calcifying every other account of life that it touched. In those inner places it drained life. The wounded Christian has been conscious of the wound for so long, nursing the pain and rehearsing the desire for justice, that their soul's orientation has turned inward. We have all known people whose whole bodies have been crippled because their minds and emotions had become fixed upon the thought that they had been sinned against or that their own sin was justifiable.

I am reminded of the courtroom scene in Shakespeare's *The Merchant of Venice*. An embittered money-lender, Shylock, has lent money to his enemy, Antonio, who has put up as collateral a "pound of flesh" that he would forfeit if he cannot repay the loan. When his business dealing fails, Antonio has fallen into Shylock's power, and the lender is ready to cut the heart from his enemy for the defaulted debt. Like Shylock demands his rights, a resentful person effectively says, "My deeds upon my head! I crave the law." But as the bitter person's wholesale self-torment shows, by craving justice, "thou shalt have justice, more than thou desirest." In other words, hunger for the justice of the Law destroys the vengeance-desiring party as much as the one needing forgiveness. It brings torment inverse to that of grace, which "is twice blest, for it blesseth him that gives and him that takes." The Law curses both him that sins and him that holds that sin against his brother. As Shakespeare urges through the mouth of his character Portia, "Though justice be thy plea, consider this, / That, in the course of justice, none of us / Should see salvation." None of us is particularly lovable, and none of us can stand before God according to the Law.

Instead of pleading our own righteousness and urging judgment on our offenders, we are commanded to forgive, remarkably, for our own good as well as theirs. In teaching his disciples to pray, Jesus said, "if you forgive others their trespasses, your heavenly Father will also forgive you, but if you do not forgive others their trespasses, neither will your Father forgive your trespasses" (Matthew 6:14–15). God only commands what is for our good, and forgiving is for everyone's good.

This radically transformative nature of forgiveness has nowhere been more astonishingly witnessed than in the stories of forgiveness and reconciliation after the Rwandan genocide. Consider our mutual friend Alex, who as a thirteen-year old was with his father when he was killed by their neighbors. During the massacre, one of the neighbors grabbed Alex and took him into his own household, where Alex spent the next five years living among his father's killers. Unable to express his feelings, nor in a situation that would allow the truth to be spoken, the darkness settled into him to the point that he became totally silent. He slipped into what appeared to be a waking coma, in which he was taken to a mental hospital. It was there that he was found by our friend Bishop Emmanuel Ngendahayo, who had become known for helping people whom no one else could help. He began speaking to Alex and praying for him. Day after day he came to the hospital, praying and telling him truth. One day the words made their way to the place where Alex had lost himself, and like a ray of light showed him a way out of the darkness. After he came to live with the bishop, Alex found that his story had to be changed. He could not demand the Law and be free. He had to forgive.

When he was able to forgive and release his desire for justice and vengeance, he himself was set free. No one could deny that he had been sinned against. No one could deny that he had been psychologically tortured for years. But none knew better than him that vengeance could never have quenched his pain or healed his wounds. The only remedy was receiving the grace of God in order to give the grace of God.

Our friend became a vessel of grace—the cleansing power of God working its way through his being. Not only was he healed of the debilitating thoughts and tormenting darkness, he was filled with the life of God. Today he is an evangelist, testifying to the transformation that comes when we acknowledge our own need for the blood of Jesus, and the truth that every human being needs mercy. But what is most remarkable about Alex is that you would never suspect the terrible pain of his life because of how thoroughly it has been eclipsed by joy. The light of God that led him out of the darkness of bitterness has remained in his heart, and joy beams out of him, continually displayed on his countenance and in every interaction. He bears the family resemblance.

QUESTIONS FOR REFLECTION

Through the Law, God gave habits of worship to his people, and such habits are obviously very helpful in forming character, but why wasn't the Law enough to make a "holy people"? Why are good habits and even good worship still not enough to make one holy?

Which of your family traits or learned patterns are hindering your growth in God's family traits? Is this a moment when you might act in self-sacrificial love for God and offer him a desire, habit, thought, or practice that you know is inconsistent with his ways?

Are you holding on to bitterness? That is a place in your heart where a spring of grace and joy is waiting to be unstopped.

6

The Simple Joy of Contentment

THE TRIUMPH OF DISCONTENTMENT

IN EIGHTEENTH-CENTURY FRANCE, DURING the age that has come to be called the Enlightenment, a philosopher named Jean-Jacques Rousseau defied the Christian tradition of Western society on one of its foundational points of agreement, that human beings are inherently wicked due to the Fall. Instead, Rousseau argued, people are inherently good; it is society that makes us bad. Taking up Rousseau's banner and his proclamation of the rightness of individual passions, Sigmund Freud gave to late modernity a vocabulary and form of justification for individualism as a total way of life. In *Civilization and Its Discontents* (1930), capping off his life's work, Freud pitted individual desires, passions, and drives against the constraining forces of society. Every person, he argues, wants to express himself as much as possible in every way possible—wants no restriction on freedoms—especially stemming from instinct-driven sexual desires. Because not everyone can satisfy these desires in community, the terrible price for living in civil society is a guilty conscience, which people experience as anxiety

The Simple Joy of Contentment

or discontent. Authority and the restrictions of custom must be heeded, but they are always resented.

Following the path of modernity that we discussed in chapter 3, Freud envisioned a new kind of society in which the need for authority would be reduced along with dependence on customs and traditions. Philip Rieff describes Freud's vision in *Triumph of the Therapeutic*: "A new kind of community could be constructed, one that did not generate conscience and internal control but desire and the safe play of impulse. From this *pneuma* pulsing through the intimate world of friendship and love, the next culture gives signs that it will emerge—a culture that would not oppose the self but express more fully its varieties."[1] Replacing the Christian ideal of a single body composed of many members united by a common Spirit, and happiness derived from submission to God and his ways, Freud argued for a cultivated, strong self-interest as the fount of happiness. Psychotherapy was his prescription for this cultivation of the self.

Although significant details of Freud's theory have been rejected even by later secular psychologists, his model of a human as "psychological man" and his focus on self-exploration has become the dominant way of thinking in Western society. Happiness, we are told, will come by getting rid of all the negative thoughts about yourself and your behavior, so that you will be free to do what you feel like and be whomever you want to be. And in a society operating with a standard of living unimagined by previous centuries, the scope for pleasure, choice, and indulgence seems limited only by the irritating necessities of work and income. We are a collection of competing individuals, striving with the problem of limited time and money to maximize happiness, understood primarily in physical and psychological terms.

As almost anyone in America knows, though, notwithstanding the triumph of the therapeutic (to borrow Rieff's phrase) late modernity has not produced more complete happiness but has spawned inventive forms of misery. News outlets from *Newsweek* to the *New York Times* report that anxiety in America is at an

---

1. Rieff, *Triumph*, 42-43.

Part II: Paths to Rediscovering Joy

all-time high. The National Institute of Mental Health has found that one third of adults suffer from anxiety disorders, and the American College Health Association shows that 62% of university undergraduates in 2016 reported "overwhelming anxiety."[2] The tumult of 2020 has only increased that figure. Whereas anxiety—a reasonable sense of stress or worry over legitimate challenges—is experienced evenly across global populations, and depression occurs similarly around the world, the World Health Organization has found that anxiety *disorders* are exceptionally common in the Americas, far outpacing every other region of the world.[3] In this assessment, the WHO includes irrational and extreme stress or fear diagnosed as General Anxiety Disorder (GAD), panic disorder, phobias, social anxiety disorder, obsessive-compulsive disorder (OCD) and post-traumatic stress disorder (PTSD). Despite having the highest standard of living the world has ever known, millions of Americans are crippled by irrational fear and worry. Freud's therapeutic society has not given its promised liberation from discontent. We should demand a refund.

No one knows or adequately understands all that has contributed to the spike in fear and anxiety in the West. Some suggest the trouble comes from our diets and genetically modified foods. Some argue that the principle cause is technology use, whether the screen itself or the behavior connected with it. Social media is frequently linked with anxiety and obsession disorders. Others argue for more direct spiritual causes, citing a nation that has rejected Christian values in order to serve the god of the Self. Whatever the mix of causes, some generalizations can be drawn that demonstrate that late modernity by its nature produces a condition of suffering.

---

2. Newman, "Anxiety in the West."
3. WHO. *Depression and Anxiety*, 7-11.

THE SIMPLE JOY OF CONTENTMENT
LIVING IN THE SHALLOWS

Throughout history, Christians have experienced the hardships of a fallen world just like their non-Christian neighbors. But late modern society presents Christians with a set of assumptions that increase the likelihood of increased suffering and of losing our way to joy.

In pre-modernity, when Christians have experienced hardship, their immediate turn was to consider spiritual causes and spiritual solutions. Indeed, one criticism of pre-modern societies past and present is that every event, good or bad, is given a spiritual cause.[4] For example, in the fight against Ebola in Congo, the virus is often considered a pawn of personal evil agents. Similarly, plagues of the past were understood to have spiritual causes, like the Babylonian god Errata or the Greek god Apollo, or offended ancestors in animist cultures. Whatever one thinks of the relative operations of microbes and demons, modernity's concentration on material causes for everything has had profound consequences in the West. Rather than consider the spiritual aspects of a personal difficulty, whether it be health-related or interpersonal, modern society has come to focus almost exclusively on what we think we understand. We have de-spiritualized the world. Indeed, a de-spiritualized worldview is one definition of modernity.

Capturing the emergent ethos of modernity back in 1922, T.S. Eliot noted the de-sacralization of the West in his poem *The Wasteland*:

> The river's tent is broken: the last fingers of leaf
> Clutch and sink into the wet bank. The wind
> Crosses the brown land, unheard. The nymphs are departed.

With the rise of scientific materialism and the dominance of a psychological explanation of Man, everything and everywhere is reduced to matter, chemicals, and what can be studied. The result is a barren land, and no spirit—only "the wind / crosses the brown land, unheard." Spiritual awareness is gone: "The nymphs are departed." Not only does this produce a pretty boring sense of the

---

4. See, for example, Jenkins, *New Faces* and *Next Christendom*; and Tennant, *Theology*, esp. chapter 5.

world and the cosmos, it has serious unintended consequences for the loss of joy.

To the degree that late modern society focuses on material causes and Western achievements, and reduces man to psychology, our culture affirms and fosters an illusion of control. From our infancy, we are constantly given the message that we can get whatever we want and become whatever we want to be. Echoing Rousseau and Freud, nothing should stand in the way of our aims and desires: not natural inequalities, not inherited differences, not even biology. If our circumstances constrain and limit, then we just need to find the material solution to satisfy our desires. If we have the wrong biology to match our thinking, then we can change even that. And if ever the messages of boundless pursuits are lacking or quietly denied, efforts are made to challenge the limitations. "Man is not limited!" our culture insists. Everything must be permitted except any attempt to imply limitation.

The power to determine ourselves, our circumstances, and our relationships is consistently assumed and celebrated as obviously essential to human happiness. In a word: control. To lack control is the late modern American's nightmare. To lack control of our future, to be stuck in a job or housing situation, or to be unable to distance ourselves from unpleasant people are all situations not to be borne. We all know many people—probably friends and members of our family—who are forever moving from job to job, church to church, hobby to hobby, or house to house in pursuit of the perfect situation that will satisfy all their longings for happiness. Christians will often cast their emotional discontent in spiritual language, claiming the Spirit has led them into each evasion of responsibility, conflict, or commitment.

These restless movements are merely indications of a deeper assumption of personal control. Rousseau's revolutionary assertion of inherent human goodness and Freud's championing of desire were easy sells in a culture deeply shaped by a belief in independence from any kind of external control. The independent spirit that seemed right for the colonies in 1776 became assumed of every person individually.

The Simple Joy of Contentment

Unfortunately for the one seeking endless happiness, control is an illusion. We cannot even control how our next meal will sit in our tummies, or whether we will sleep well tonight. Chances are very high that one of the next three people I talk to will have a headache or have had a bad morning, so that our interaction will not meet my expectations. If I cannot control the outcomes of my meals, sleep, or conversations, how little can I hope to control matters of larger import or longer duration? It seems obvious upon slight examination that seeking to control our lives and other people will lead to frustration, misery, and joylessness. To say it another way, though, the pursuit of control causes our own suffering.

In contemporary late modernity, the suffering from frustrated control has grown new tools through technology. By its nature, technology is developed to make things faster and easier, and to eliminate the unpredictable and uncontrollable. Ovens are better than fires; microwaves are better than ovens. A phone call eliminates the hassles, negotiations, and duration of a visit; a text eliminates the social niceties, subtleties, and planning of a phone call. Electronic checkouts at the grocery, ATMs, and automated ordering are all designed to avoid direct social contact and the vulnerabilities inherent in conversation. While it is assumed but never stated, if we can avoid vulnerability, we can remain in control.

In no arena is the will to control more apparent than in the online virtual world. In *The Second Self* and *Alone Together*, MIT philosopher Sherry Turkle has written extensively on the self-defeating effects of personal electronic devices and social media. Holding out the promise of constant connection, we have never been more isolated. In her phrase, we are "alone together." The aloneness tends to derive from a desire to manage a public image. By creating a "second self" or a "virtual self," I can craft and control a persona that highlights what is going well and hides what is not. My idealized second self may resemble me only slightly. To the extent that my second self is well-liked (by other virtual selves) and achieves some arbitrarily measured form of success, this second self may be happier and freer than my actual self. With this second self, nothing can destroy my illusion of control because the technological image is, in matter of fact, under my control. Despite the ability to fashion a digital persona and interact with others almost exclusively through it, many people experience debilitating anxiety *for the virtual self* and its image, whether it is well-liked, and whether it garners attention. But of course, it can always be changed and created afresh. Technology has turned metaphors about image management into (virtual) reality.

So why so much misery? Why so much anxiety when Western culture makes ever more control seem possible?

Because we were not made to be in control. God made us with a place in a hierarchy, to rule creation but to be ruled by him. Any control we exercise—whether over our own bodies or over our environment—was to be exercised under his authority and according to what he has revealed as his will. To exercise individual control based upon personal inclination is not only arbitrary, but it inevitably brings conflict with others' aims and desires. On the other hand, when we make decisions for our bodies and environments based on what God has revealed, we have the possibility of peace because we are following a common lead. Imagine a team of eight rowing a boat. If each one closes his eyes and ears and rows to his own beat, how well will the boat move? But if each crew member listens to the coxswain and watches the rower in front of him, they can move the boat with synchronous power.

Sadly, Western Christians who live within this cultural environment have unconsciously absorbed these assumptions and resist the idea of yielding control. It is not only secular people who seek happiness in maximum comfort with minimal limitations on control. Similarly, Christians ignore spiritual causes of their discontent because those causes seem too mysterious or unmanageable; indeed, they are beyond our immediate control. When we encounter a hardship, fear, discomfort, or conflict, we tend to rush to what will make us feel better or most quickly relieve tension rather than what will address our sin, the sins committed against us, or the hold of evil based on those sins. Seeking the healing and power of the Holy Spirit is often a last resort.

The Simple Joy of Contentment

SURRENDER AND CONTENTMENT

The modern model of "psychological man" ignores a crucial reality: to be human is to have a spirit and to live according to spiritual realities. This condition is not an option for Christians. The inner being of each and every person was made to interact with the unseen God and to receive life and strength from him. God has put his Holy Spirit in his people in order shape their life, outlook, values, and affections. In short, his Spirit is given to restore the design of a human to its integrated whole, relating rightly to self, others, and God. But to the degree that a person lives with reference to external inputs as sources of happiness (clicks, likes, and comments), and measures a good life and well-being by circumstances and emotions, he will live with decreasing reference to the Holy Spirit and the indwelling Word.

As we discussed in chapter 1, we were designed to live under the rule of God and with constant reference to him. We were made for the indwelling Word to give participation in the life of God and in his right understanding of the world. All goodness flows from him, and obedience to his ways brings deep pleasure to the inner being of a person. The rule of God brings joy. The only path for a modern Christian to find joy is the same path that has been offered to God's people at all times and all places: surrender control.

Surrender is costly. While it requires an act of will, surrender also implies and assumes the active work of the Holy Spirit who is ready to bring order to the chaotic human mind and heart. Nevertheless, the act of surrender always costs. In particular, the act of surrender requires that we turn from our submission to one faulty source of hope and strength in order to submit to God. Or to say it another way, we must relinquish our deep affection for something or someone that has become a substitute for God, including an affection for an ideal vision of ourselves.

Consider Jesus as he taught a group of people whose lives were every bit as full of fear and worry as our own. As recorded in Matthew, Mark, and Luke, Jesus is looking across a crowd of first century peasants. Many of the people are barefoot; their clothes are worn out and patched. Jesus himself is wearing the one tunic and mantle he owns. For all of them, food is a matter of daily concern. And this loving teacher, who shares their situation, looks across their faces and says, "Do not worry about your life, what you will eat, nor about your body, what you will put on. For life is more than food, and the body more than clothing." He elaborates his point with examples of God's constant care, how he clothes the lilies of the field and knows each and every sparrow. And of course, he reminds them, you are of more value than these, and God knows what you need. Then he comes back to the point: "So do not seek what you are to eat and what you are to drink, nor be worried. For all the nations of the world seek after these things, and your Father knows that you need them" (Luke 12:29–30).

Jesus has a way of bringing up what he knows to be typical ways of thinking or acting, or standard teachings and default responses. He raises the norms we tend to think are important or good for us and then publicly challenges them. Often it is the stuff of unexamined assumption and social norms, what we often call *culture* because it is the ground and nourishment that *cultivates* or grows us in a society. Jesus critiques culture by raising the norms and then countering those with what *he* says is truly for our good. In these moments, he often begins, "Truly, truly I say to you."

The norm for that crowd of peasants, he knew, was to be troubled and consumed with what to eat, what to wear, and how to improve the circumstances of everyday life. They were supremely interested in "our daily bread." Were he speaking to a contemporary crowd of Western Christians steeped in the cultivation of modernity, he would raise different norms that trouble us. He would speak to the concerns of psychological man. He would probably raise the tendency to want just a bit more—a bit bigger home, a bit nicer car, a bit more financial cushion, more time, more opportunity for vacation and recreation, more eating out. Succinctly put, consumption. In the history of the world, there has never been a society that consumes like ours, thirsty to satisfy our need for meaning. Even though our norms are different than this crowd in ancient Israel, Jesus's critical counterpoint stands. Instead of seeking what the nations seek, "seek his kingdom, and these things will be added to you. Do not be afraid, little flock, for it is your Father's good pleasure to give you the kingdom" (Luke 12:31–32). Jesus brings a word from the realms of heaven. It is gentle, but it is a bolt of contrast. You have been given the everlasting kingdom of God, he declares. What more could you want?

Jesus knows what is good for people—what is really and truly good for us—and he wants us to truly want what will nourish us. He pushes towards the contrast that cuts to our hearts. In Luke 12:32–34, he says, "It is your Father's good pleasure to give you the kingdom. Sell your possessions, and give to the needy. Provide yourselves with moneybags that do not grow old, with a treasure in the heavens that does not fail, where no thief approaches and no moth destroys. For where your treasure is, there will your heart be also." Here is the cost of surrender. Jesus designed and created human beings, so he knows what happens when we fix our attentions and set our hearts on things that are dying.

By design, we are made to seek approval, to want to feel safe, to feel significant and important, to order and organize our environment, to feel pleasure through our bodies, to have our minds alert with learning, and to feel happy, content, and at peace. Those are all part of the design from the beginning; they are part of the kingdom of heaven. But they were all given with primary reference to God our Father. Approval, safety, and significance were to come from him, along with the commission to learn his world and order it, enjoying it and each other under his rule, with the designed result of joy.

But when we seek those things from something or someone that is not God, we make gods out of them. The trouble becomes serious quickly because if it is not God, then it is something in the process of dying. By dying, we mean it is part of the temporary world that is perishing. When we look for approval, significance, or meaning from something that is dying, we give it (or him or her) a role it was never meant to have, so it grows in our hearts out of proportion. Looking to and trusting in things that are dying is like one drowning person trying to be saved by another drowning person—grasping, clutching, overwhelming. Money, power, status, reputation, bodily pleasure, a career . . . they promise so much in the short term, but when we trust in them, they grow out of proportion. Lacking inherent life and desperately brief, those dying things tend to overwhelm and require full attention.

In 1 John 2:15 and following, John echoes Jesus, "Do not love the world or the things in the world. If anyone loves the world, the love of the Father is not in him. For all that is in the world—the desires of the flesh and the desires of the eyes and pride of life—is not from the Father but is from the world. And the world is passing away along with its desires, but whoever does the will of God abides forever." If the object of your affections is of the world, then it is dying—passing away—and it can neither satisfy your longings nor provide what you are hoping it will provide. With a terrible irony, even the many good things of this dying world go bad on us when we put our hope and significance in them.

Jesus's solution to our problem is radical: "It is your Father's good pleasure to give you the kingdom. Sell your possessions, and give to the needy. Provide yourselves with moneybags that do not grow old, with a treasure in the heavens that does not fail, where no thief approaches and no moth destroys. Where your treasure is, there will your heart be also" (Luke 12:33–34). You have the kingdom, he says! Your heart will be in what you hope for and trust in, so get rid of whatever sets itself up as of greater value, as a supreme treasure. Sometimes we rationalize our divided loyalties, thinking we can maintain allegiance to God and devotion to some other pursuit or person. But the affections of the heart are limited, and our capacity to organize and align our thoughts is limited. Our time and energy are limited, as is our emotional capacity to develop and maintain relationship. As dependent creatures, we are fundamentally limited.

Jesus reveals that contentment comes when we choose his kingdom and live with principal regard to it. When God takes the first place, he causes the lesser things—good things but dying things—to take their right order. They can be enjoyed in the proportion for which they were given. This idea of proportion or order is what he means with "Seek first the kingdom, and these things will be added to you." Rather than being consumed endlessly by job, money, relationships, status, pleasure, house, and comforts, giving them up to the direction of God renders them powerless over us. These things were given to be our helpful servants, but they make terrible masters. Because God has brought us into his kingdom, we no longer have to be slaves of consumption or seekers after a dying happiness. Modernity and its discontentment is not the preferred option.

When we accept the way of contentment by seeking the kingdom, Jesus says we will find ourselves storing up treasure in heaven. Sometimes people think they will store up treasure in heaven by giving money to good causes or to missions. While that may be one of the means by which the Lord helps us to sacrifice love for money, storing up heavenly treasure is opening yourself to more of God's kingdom filling you. He is the treasure; the perfect being; the only good one; the fountain of all goodness. By turning our affection to God, he grows our capacity for more of him. He alone is the treasure. Jesus says, "It's your Father's good pleasure to give you the kingdom"; seek him; open your heart, your attention, and your awareness to him. He then opens you. A good measure of treasure, heaped up, overflowing, will be poured into your heart.

When we surrender our attempts at control and the single-minded pursuit of temporal happiness, we accept God's design for us. Rather than battling the restrictions on our pleasures that we inevitably encounter every day, we can accept that God is the ruler of his world, including us. And what's more, he cares for us. He knows what we need, and we can trust him to provide what is ultimately needed for meaning and significance. We do not have to strive to make our lives matter because he has already given us everlasting importance. We are known by our Creator, and we have important work to do in his household. In this surrender to the plans and purposes of God, there is a deep well of contentment that never runs dry.

QUESTIONS FOR REFLECTION

Have you believed that there is something missing in your life that, if only you could get it, would finally make you happy and bring fulfillment? Consider offering it to the Lord and whether you may need to repent of an idolatry.

What role does social media play in your life? Does it draw you closer to God and lift your heart? What vision of your life does it feed?

Instead of feeding devotion to the self and to what is perishing, how might you develop appetites of your soul for the things of God that will last forever?

7

The Joy of Serving in the Kingdom

CELESTIN IS A LOCAL farmer in Gisenyi, Rwanda, who is really good at growing Irish potatoes (or russets if you are an American). Using innovative methods, he would regularly grow twenty tons a season, twice as many as any other single farmer could manage. After attending a church seminar on using your gifts for the kingdom of God, he wanted to purposely serve the kingdom. Growing up in the church, he had come to believe (whether or not he had been taught it explicitly) that real Christian service is only for pastors who were called to serve the church. After attending the seminar, he began to think about his knowledge of farming as a treasure (like the talent in Jesus's parable) given to be stewarded and used for the kingdom. He started showing other people how to grow Irish potatoes using his insightful techniques. Many young people who were desperate to find a job came to learn from him. Each one would work for him for a short time, and then he would give them their own start, never concerned about competition. His village is now known as the most important center for Irish potatoes in the western part of Rwanda. People will travel from across the country to meet Celestin and discover how this village came to be so prosperous. He always says the same thing: knowledge and skill are gifts of the Lord. Sometimes he is asked to preach, and his typical encouragement is to make everything God gave you into a tool for serving his people. In the long run, by realizing that his work belonged to God, he was able to see that it belonged to his community as much as to him, and he discovered overflowing joy to serve his people with all his heart.

Celestin has recovered something core to his design. Recalling the design for creation that we discussed in chapter 1, service is one of the essential components of a healthy relationship with God. In Genesis 2:7–8, 15, we read, "then the LORD God formed the man of dust from the ground and breathed into his nostrils the breath of life, and the man became a living creature. And the LORD God planted a garden in Eden, in the east, and there he put the man whom he had formed. . . . The LORD God took the man and put him in the garden of Eden to work it and keep it." In the Garden, God gave Adam and Eve the simple task of stewarding a responsive garden. His Word lived in them and gave an intuitive understanding of the creation. When Adam named all the creatures, he was demonstrating his divine image-bearing, creatively speaking in accordance with the wisdom of God. In other words, he named them accurately, for in the presence of God, "whatever the man called every living creature, that was its name" (Gen 2:19). Working together, Adam with Eve tended the garden with this same Spirit-filled knowledge of the creation. Along with intuitive knowledge from the Word, God seemingly equipped them with ever-deepening experiential knowledge. As they labored according to the knowledge of God, they were given a way to serve God and thereby express their appreciation for the Creator and what he had given them.

Genesis also reveals that God regularly visited them personally, walking with them in the Garden in the cool of the day. Such visits were an opportunity for a unique kind of worship. Part of the joy of serving is presenting the fruits of our labors to the one for whom the work is done. The divine visitations were a moment to say, "Look what we did! See how we trained this vine to climb this tree!" or perhaps, with a note of celebration, "We just discovered how you made this amazing monkey to eat this kind of fruit, so that it spreads the seeds to new parts of the garden!" When our labors of mind and body are acknowledged by the one we adore, and when we know we are valued, even difficult tasks bring joy and delight with them. Taken together, their service and its reception rendered it worship. Through their work they could tangibly express the "worthiness" of God, which is at the root of our word "worship"—"worth-ship." What God had done in creation was supremely worthy, and their good work in his honor was deemed worthy by their loving Lord.

Today, many in the church around the world use the word worship to refer either to the time of singing songs of praise, or to the God-focused attitude of the gathering. Worship is thus bracketed in time and with reference to specific activities. While the singing of praise is certainly worship, as is the corporate gathering of God's people to remember, celebrate, praise, and thank God for his redemptive work, worship can also characterize many more facets of a Christian's life, not least service. Since our original design included service as a primary way to acknowledge the worth of God and his gifts, service remains a deeply embedded way through which we can worship God and, as a result, it can fill us with the joy of living our design. To borrow from Aristotle, true happiness comes by acting in accordance with the end of a human's design, and to worship through service is living according to the chief end for which we were made.[1] When Celestine works the ground, plants and tends potatoes, and then passes on that wisdom with grateful acknowledgement of God, he is worshiping through service and living the design for mankind.

---

1. See Aristotle's *Nicomachean Ethics*, where eudaemonia, or happiness, is described as "something final and self-sufficient, and an end [telos] of all action" (Book 1.7), and it is achieved through "activity of soul in accordance with perfect virtue" (Book I.13).

Part II: Paths to Rediscovering Joy

THE RESTORATION OF SERVICE

Each of us knows the frustration of working endlessly to get something we want or believe we need. It is a common story for writers, athletes, or artists to give thousands of hours to a project or goal, and upon achieving it, to fall into deep depression and hopelessness. Expecting achievement to deliver happiness, instead it proved to be a gilded shell, an empty cup. For others, we strive to make a business succeed, grow a church, find a fulfilling relationship, get enough money, or finally be respected. Again and again, honest people report that attaining these goals, simply as ends in themselves or for the end of personal happiness, is never enough. Spending ourselves on ourselves—our life, energy, and resources—will only empty us out. Instead, we were made to spend ourselves for the sake of others and the honor of the One who gave us everything.

Part of Christ's redemptive work was to give back to mankind both the knowledge and ability to serve God according to the original design. As the true Man, the second Adam, Jesus Christ reunited the Word of God to human nature: "for if, because of one man's trespass, death reigned through that one man, much more will those who receive the abundance of grace and the free gift of righteousness reign in life through the one man Jesus Christ. . . . For the death he died, he died to sin, once for all, but the life he lives he lives to God" (Rom 5:17, 6:10). Having dealt with Adam's original sin and the consequent enslavement to the flesh, Jesus broke the bonds of human captivity to sin so that God's life and righteousness might rule in a human life. The Word of God can dwell within a human heart again, the renovation of design. As we saw with Adam and Eve in the Garden, when the Word dwells within, he teaches how to worship through service.

Jesus is again the model for what a restored person looks like when worshiping through service. The Apostle Paul explains it well in Philippians 2:1–8:

> So if there is any encouragement in Christ, any comfort from love, any participation in the Spirit, any affection

and sympathy, complete my joy by being of the same mind, having the same love, being in full accord and of one mind. Do nothing from selfish ambition or conceit, but in humility count others more significant than yourselves. Let each of you look not only to his own interests, but also to the interests of others. Have this mind among yourselves, which is yours in Christ Jesus, who, though he was in the form of God, did not count equality with God a thing to be grasped, but emptied himself, by taking the form of a servant, being born in the likeness of men. And being found in human form, he humbled himself by becoming obedient to the point of death, even death on a cross.

Countless books have been written on this passage, but the point we wish to identify is that when God takes human form, it is in order to serve for the sake of others – even his enemies – and "to give his life as a ransom for many" (Matt 20:28). A perfected human is one who humbles himself completely and obeys God to the most extreme extent. Although he did not delight in the suffering itself and even wished to avoid it, the perfect Man was chiefly interested in the eternal interests of others. He served "for the life of the world" (John 6:51). As the Philippians passage teaches, those who are in Christ, who have been wakened by the Spirit, are therefore urged to have this same mind, "which is yours in Christ Jesus." In other words, to live according to the restored design, we also must serve with a mind towards the interests of others. Instead of working and laboring for the end of our own happiness, the mind of Christ leads us to ignore ambition and conceit. As we can see by looking at Christ's example, the renewal of life flows out when we serve in this way.

The kingdom grows when restored people serve in the power of God's Spirit. God has given his gifts not to those who will spend them on themselves, but to those who will spend themselves in order to give to others.

Part II: Paths to Rediscovering Joy

GIFTS AND TALENTS

Modern Pentecostalism often narrows the gifts of the Holy Spirit to supernatural demonstration like performing miracles, casting out demons, and speaking in tongues. For some the impulse is towards visibly legitimizing the kingdom of Christ as it pushes into the territories of the kingdom of darkness, while for others the demonstration of legitimacy concerns the person exercising the gifts. A true Christian, on this account, will speak in tongues and perform works of spiritual power. Another dimension of insisting on these more demonstrative gifts is that they are useful. Healing and deliverance from demonic oppression feel especially pressing in areas without adequate healthcare and with spiritual warfare being waged against sorcerers.

We certainly acknowledge the value of gifts of healing, the encouragement of speaking in tongues, and the necessity of deliverance from demons, but an absolute emphasis on these outwardly manifesting gifts limits the scope of the biblical gifts in general and tends towards the overall weakening of the church body. A more faithful treatment of biblical wisdom needs to incorporate spiritual gifts into a broader understanding of serving Christ's body in the power of the Holy Spirit. In Paul's explanation of gifts in Ephesians, he cites the very public ministerial gifts as given for the benefit of all: "And He gave some as apostles, and some as prophets, and some as evangelists, and some as pastors and teachers, for the equipping of the saints for the work of service, to the building up of the body of Christ" (Eph 4:10–12). But the upbuilding of the body includes and even requires all sorts of gifts, as evident in his letter to Rome: "we have many members in one body and all the members do not have the same function, so we, who are many, are one body in Christ, and individually members one of another. And since we have gifts that differ according to the grace given to us, let each exercise them accordingly: if prophecy, according to the proportion of his faith; if service, in his serving; or he who teaches, in his teaching; or he who exhorts, in his exhortation; he who gives, with liberality; he who leads, with diligence; he who shows mercy, with cheerfulness" (Rom 12:3–7). In the same thought are included teaching and mercy, prophecy and giving. Everything we have is a gift from God, whether our faith, knowledge, understanding, creativity, compassion, and insight, or our ability to lead, preach, teach, evangelize, serve, manage, and encourage. Every gathering of local believers needs wisdom in all sorts of areas to sustain life together over time, especially if they wish to minister to surrounding people and share the gospel of Jesus. The bottom line is expressed in 1 Corinthians, "one and the same Spirit works all these things, distributing to each one individually just as He wills" (1 Cor 12.11).

Gifts are given for the building up of the whole body, not for the exaltation of the self. Having the mind of Christ in the exercise of gifting means using them humbly for the benefit of all, not with ambition to bring glory to the self. When we follow God's design for the use of his spiritually empowered service, great joy accompanies the service.

Consider Moses's account of God's instructions for the Tabernacle. God ordered Moses to seek those whom God had anointed with the gifts of craftsmanship. Then the Lord said to Moses,

> "See, I have chosen Bezalel son of Uri, the son of Hur, of the tribe of Judah, and I have filled him with the Spirit of God, with wisdom, with understanding, with knowledge and with all kinds of skills—to make artistic designs for work in gold, silver and bronze, to cut and set stones, to work in wood, and to engage in all kinds of crafts. Moreover, I have appointed Oholiab son of Ahisamak, of the tribe of Dan, to help him. Also I have given ability to all the skilled workers to make everything I have commanded you: the tent of meeting, the ark of the covenant law with the atonement cover on it, and all the other furnishings of the tent."

In a very explicit way, God communicates that he has given practical wisdom, understanding, and knowledge for the construction of the Tabernacle, so that the people could draw near to God in ways that would instil fitting honor for him. It would be a beautiful place that would encourage appropriate awe and wonder in accord with the awesome and wonderful God who met them there. The space itself, as well as the rituals of worship, would teach the people about him and about their relationship to him. It was for God's honor and for his worship, but the craftsmen were given the joy and privilege of participating in its establishment. Like Adam and Eve presenting their work to God in the Garden, whenever we use our gifts to please God, we experience his smiling delight as an inner burning of joy.

SERVE AS IF SERVING OUR LORD IN HEAVEN

The fallen condition offers a rival plan to the joy that flows from God's pleasure in our work. The self-focused plan for work offers more immediate and often more tangibly rewarding results: the honor and admiration of men. When I entered life in the church as a new convert from Islam, I (Cedric) wanted to see passionate activity for the glory of God and leaders challenging the apathy of church members. But I kept seeing stagnation. Before long I realized that the church is just as subject to the temptations of the world as those without the Spirit, including the temptation to seek personal honor from men. But we have the added temptation of whitewashing our sin, or giving it a spiritualized justification. One of the teachings most churches accept is that you should obey and respect those in authority over you, such as your bishop, district superintendent, presbytery, or elder board (depending on your ecclesial structure). To my dismay, I found that many clergy shaped their life and work around pleasing the bishop instead of doing the pastoral work they vowed to perform. Many pastors would neglect their congregants and their preaching in order to do special projects for the bishop. They kept in their eye the possibility of climbing a ladder of influence within the church, and keeping in the good graces of the bishop was necessary to get the best appointments. Over time, I have encountered the sad fact that this is a problem in every denomination. Pastors vie for influence in order to get larger or more prestigious church appointments, as well as more public platforms.

Traveling in America, I have seen a special form of this man-pleasing corruption. Pastors seek a kind of celebrity status, gaining followers on social media or through blogs as if they are professional athletes or popstars. Like secular celebrities, these celebrity pastors make public comments on every issue, as if they have been given special insight from God into the fallen affairs of a perishing order. They justify their ceaseless activity with the thought that they are reaching more people for Christ. On this account, it seems Christ is unable to use the weak things of the world to shame the strong; it seems he is unable to use his local church in all its simplicity; it seems he is dependent on the winsome and clever speaker with good looks. I find myself wondering how they keep the name of pastor when they are insulated from the sheep. Taking assurance from Jesus's words that the sheep know the sound of the shepherd's voice—and they sure talk enough to be heard by all—they seem to have forgotten that he also said, "I know my sheep and my sheep know me" (John 10:14). If a pastor takes seriously his calling as a shepherd of sheep, whom he must know in order to guide, then he will seek to please the one who called him and gave him the task of caring for the sheep.

Ironically, we can confront our spiritualizing tendency and learn something from the secular world. Just as Jesus taught in the parable of the shrewd manager, "the people of this world are more shrewd in dealing with their own kind than are the people of the light" (Luke 16:8). He gives a lesson about serving wisely through clarity about whom you are serving and the ends you hope to attain. People without hope of heaven work in this world to maximize what they can get in this life, so they seek to please those who can benefit them. Somehow, Christians quickly forget that eternal benefits come from pleasing the Lord of Eternity. A wise and shrewd Christian would seek to please the Lord of All, who holds the storehouse of rewards.

I have seen the contrast often. In Rwanda there is a Christian retreat center where I go two times a year for a prayer retreat.

Part II: Paths to Rediscovering Joy

One time I had been in prayer and wanted to write down some thoughts, but the battery in my computer was failing and I had forgotten my power cord. Everyone I approached for help was hostile. A lady at the reception desk first tried to ignore me, pretending to be focused on her computer screen. But when my stubborn presence finally compelled attention, she not only offered no help but scolded me for forgetting what I needed. I began thinking this would probably be my last visit to this place. Just as I was turning away with a heavy heart, there came a young man I mentored while he was in the university.

He greeted me with honor, "How are you, Papa?" and turning to the girl, "This is my pastor who I told you about in the workshop, whom God used to change my life."

The girl who was treating me unfairly was shocked and speechless. In an innocent voice, she asked, "Now, what was it you were asking me, sir?"

The person who called me papa was one of the shareholders of the retreat center. I asked him if it is their policy to help visitors who have needs, such as forgetting an item. He answered it is one the primary duties of the staff. The girl was anxious and fretting, knowing she was caught in her neglect, but I gave her the computer without saying anything. In order to cover her mistake, she quickly gave me the chair, saying eagerly, "Sir, you can work from here. I know you will be comfortable." The service here was presuming upon the goodwill of Christian visitors. They lacked shrewdness, forgetting that their service to clients was also a way to offer service to God. I was grieved that other people were likely being treated badly but did not have someone they knew to speak for them.

On a later occasion I decided to test how a non-Christian place operates, which makes no pretension of serving God. I went to a place near Lake Kivu, which is a secular resort. Everything was very professional. I got everything on time, and if I needed something, it took a matter of seconds. Their language was so kind that even if they couldn't give me something, they softened the disappointment with gentle language. The mission of this place was strictly profit, with the expressed goal of pleasing people. But they were preserved from the hypocrisy of pretending like they were trying to please God. They were shrewd.

Jesus follows up the parable of the shrewd manager by saying, "Whoever can be trusted with very little can also be trusted with much, and whoever is dishonest with very little will also be dishonest with much. So if you have not been trustworthy in handling worldly wealth, who will trust you with true riches? And if you have not been trustworthy with someone else's property, who will give you property of your own?" (Luke 16:10–12). When people of the kingdom do not use their gifts and resources to work in ways that honor God, they are not being trustworthy. They reveal that their hopes and attentions are set on the perishing world rather than investing in the kingdom that lasts forever. In all that we do, in whatever our occupation, we are to work as if we are serving God, because we really are. We are serving as his stewards, as guardians of all that he has entrusted to us.

SERVING TO THE HONOR OF GOD

One of the most widely known Christian-themed films, *Chariots of Fire*, tells the story of the Scottish rugby star and sprinter Eric Liddell. At the 1924 Olympics in Paris, Liddell refused to run in the 100-meter race in which he was highly favoured due to his conviction about Sabbath observance. Instead, he was slotted into the 400-meters. Despite previously modest times in the 400-meters, he was inspired by a note handed him just before the race, which read, "In the old book it says: 'He that honours me I will honour.'" Positioned in the outside lane, Liddell never saw the other runners, shattered his own personal best, and set an Olympic and World Record. The film beautifully captures the spirit with which Liddell approached not only running but all of life. Explaining his motivation to a crowd, he says, "God made me for a purpose, but he also made me fast. And when I run, I feel his pleasure. . . . Where does the power come from to see the race to its end? From within." His words are as succinct an explanation of joy as one could find.

When I run, I feel his pleasure. He felt joy—the smile of God and his delight—flowing in his soul as he used God's gift in a way that brought honor to God rather than to himself. Yes, thousands of people were glad to see him win the gold medal for Britain, but his joy came from pleasing God.

What the film cannot fully capture is that Liddell's commitment to serve God in all of life, through all his gifts, was put to the ultimate test. While Liddell was serving as a missionary in China following his Olympic triumph, the Japanese invaded China and imprisoned all Westerners. Among other prisoners with him at Shantung Compound, Langdon Gilkey recounted how completely Liddell lived according to his faith, despite the intense pressures of life in the camp. Gilkey famously wrote that while others, including other missionaries, acted selfishly and formed factions within the camp, Liddell was "absorbed, weary and interested, pouring all of himself into this effort to capture the imagination of these penned-up youths. He was overflowing with good humour and love for life, and with enthusiasm and charm. It is rare indeed that a person has the good fortune to meet a saint, but he came as close to it as anyone I have ever known."[2]

I (Ben) know of a couple who was married by Eric Liddell while imprisoned at Weixian Internment Camp (the official name of Shantung Compound). They echo Gilkey's representation of both the camp and Liddell's exemplary faith. Although he could not do the task for which he had come to China, he did everything he could do as if serving Christ. And that service was touched by the joy of the Lord because he knew the pleasure of the Lord. Even in his last days of life, he could still say, "Where does the power come from to see the race to its end? From within." The joy of the Lord was his strength.

---

2. Gilkey. *Shantung,* 192.

QUESTIONS FOR REFLECTION

Do you think about your daily routines and work as worship? How might you remind yourself during the day that your activities can be oriented to the "worth-ship" of God your Maker and Redeemer?

Take stock of the gifts, skills, and resources God has given you. Is there a new way you can serve even just *one* other person with *one* of these gifts?

Jesus speaks often about heavenly rewards for those who serve well, and he tells us it would be shrewd to work towards those rewards. Do you ever think about those rewards? If not, why not?

8

The Joy of Agreeing with God: Confession

SEVERAL YEARS AGO, I (Ben) got to know an old Welshman named William who lived for many years in Myanmar with a mission of bringing encouragement and support to churches in isolated areas, like an Onesiphorus to Paul. During one of his visits to a group of rural villages, the local pastors organized a large joint meeting for evangelism. It proved to be a season in which the Holy Spirit worked in remarkable ways, with many people giving their lives to Jesus while Christians were finding freedom from patterns of sin and fear. Like other times of refreshing such as the Welsh Revival and the East African Revival, they embraced the same empowering principle that "if we walk in the light as He is in the light, we have fellowship with one another, and the blood of Jesus His Son cleanses us from all sin" (1 John 1:7). Night after night, Christians who had lived defeated lives or had been at odds with other believers came to the meetings and openly confessed their sins. Forgiveness flooded through the gatherings, and people were filled with the Holy Spirit and with joy.

But there was a small group William noticed for whom the meetings brought no joy, and one evening they came to him after the meeting broke up. This group was frustrated because they

The Joy of Agreeing with God: Confession

were not experiencing any change in their lives. Several were new believers and had accepted the truth of Jesus, and others had been part of the church for many years, but collectively they were not feeling the life of Christ or the joy of the Lord. That night William laid his hands on each one and prayed that he or she might receive the Holy Spirit. He encouraged them to wait and see. The next night, most of them returned joyfully, sharing that they had felt the irresistible urge to go tell a family member about Jesus—to make the good confession—and immediately they were flooded with joy. And yet, a few others returned with continued discouragement.

William prayed with them again that night, encouraging them to speak out anything the Lord brought to their minds. Slowly, he asked questions about their lives, especially about how they had behaved towards the animistic spirits that had governed them before coming to Christ. As they talked, William found they had wavered between allegiances, some for many years. He urged them to verbally renounce those other powers and claim Jesus as the one Lord. There was a flurry of activity, with a few people crying out in relief and joy while at the same time others were flailing and shouting as demons resisted letting go of their captives. The claims of Christ triumphed, and the evening ended with floods of joyful praise. That is, for all except one, who was as dismayed and frustrated as could be. William asked him to come back for the last night of the planned gatherings so that they could explore one more thing.

The next day William asked around the man's village to find out anything he may not have shared. It did not take many conversations before a theme emerged. The man had been a notorious thief before his conversion, and although he no longer stole, people in his village could point at his house and identify items here and there that had once belonged to them. When the man came to the meeting, William took him aside and told him what he had discovered. The man admitted his life of theft, but stressed that it was all behind him. When William told him he needed to return what he had stolen, the fellow was indignant. No, he insisted, he had left that life, and his new life began the day of his conversion as if the old life never was. William urged him that his new King commanded reconciliation and restoration, but the man denied the claim. He could not give up the comforts he had gained through sin. He wanted to receive the salvation of Jesus the Savior, but he refused the ways of Jesus the Lord. As William put it, he was half converted, and the joy of the Lord could not be his.

When William told me this story, I realized that I have seen it countless times in Western congregations. It was my own story for many years through my youth and young manhood. Like many who grow up in the church, I never doubted the truth of the gospel, that God became man in order to save men, that he died on the Cross and rose victorious from the grave. I was glad that he offered forgiveness of sins to all who believe, and comforted myself that I was counted among them. But until a direct encounter with the holy presence of the Lord, in which my submission was made a point of order, I had subconsciously avoided obedience to Jesus as a matter of daily concern. Another way of putting it is that I had refused to agree with Jesus about my sin, and more generally, I was not interested in what Jesus thought about anything. Crucially, I found that agreeing with Jesus about our sin is a non-negotiable piece of our restoration, and there is no joy without it. We call this confession.

A MODEL CONFESSION

The essential necessity of confession for the people of God is evident by its continual appearance throughout the history of redemption. For people to experience the restoration of God's design, including its subjective feeling of joy, there has to be confession. Whether it is Abraham's agreement with God about his absolute rights over his family (Gen 22), or Moses's intercession for those terribly wavering newly adopted Israelites (Exod 32, Num 14), or the repentance of any king who walked in the humble ways of David (2 Chr 6–7, 30, 35), agreement with God about human sin and his justified condemnation regularly becomes a turning point for restoration and the realization of joy. The case of Israel's return

The Joy of Agreeing with God: Confession

from exile and the reestablishment of Jerusalem under Nehemiah's governorship is instructive.

Israel had become a people who had lost their identity as the nation with whom the Almighty God dwells. After the Babylonian King Nebuchadnezzar had conquered Judah and reconstituted the kingdom as a subjected people, King Zedekiah's rebellion prompted Nebuchadnezzar to destroy the kingdom of Judah so that it could never again rebel. He "burned the house of God and broke down the wall of Jerusalem and burned all its palaces with fire and destroyed all its precious vessels. He took into exile in Babylon those who had escaped from the sword, and they became servants to him and to his sons" (2 Chr 36:20-21). With the Temple burned and in ruins, the obvious conclusion seemed to be that God was not dwelling with his people. According to the covenant God had made with Israel at Mt. Sinai—the terms of their adoption—they would be his people and he would be their God, which would be apparent because he would be with them, go with them, and dwell with them. "God with us" was the core identity feature of this people. But with the Temple destroyed and the glory of God having departed Israel, it was no longer clear what it meant to be an Israelite or Judean.

For many of the Judeans, who came to be called Jews, the exile in Babylon became a time of grappling for a new sense of identity apart from the Temple and the Law. Where the rhythms of life had been guided by festivals and Temple observance, life in Babylon seemed rudderless, with confusion about truth and how to approach God apart from place. God had faithfully fulfilled his side of the covenant, including the promised judgments, and they had failed in their side. With no Temple to which they might turn, even those desiring to remain a distinct people in Babylon struggled to understand how to return to their side of the covenant. For some, connection to God through his Word written became the center of their identity. It was there in Babylon that the Books of Moses were brought together with later parts of their story—with the books of the Prophets and the historical chronicles of the kingdoms. Although it was not a pretty story on the human side of

95

things, still it was their story recorded in the inspired Word, and through it God was shown to be worthy of all worship. For others, though, Jewish identity became reduced to dietary distinctions, circumcision, kinship, and blood lines, as evident from the book of Esther. For these, Jewishness largely meant descent from Abraham and connection to the land of Judah. The Temple, the Covenant, and the Word were all but forgotten. Nevertheless, the Lord stood by his promises and the prophecies he had given through his servants, and after seventy years, Cyrus the Persian allowed captives to return to Jerusalem.

Nearly a hundred years after exiles began returning to Judah, Nehemiah was cupbearer to the Persian king, and upon hearing news that the returned Jews in Jerusalem were living with "trouble and shame," he asked for the king's permission and authority to bring order to God's people in their promised land. The first seven chapters of Nehemiah recount the trials and eventual success of his rebuilding program. Although a new temple had been built and consecrated by the first wave of returned exiles decades before, the people were still languishing. Walls to the city had been lacking, but something more fundamental, more foundational needed to be restored.

As told in Nehemiah chapter ten, on the first day of the seventh month, all the people assemble in the public square, and Ezra the priest brings out the Book of the Law of Moses. Standing on a platform, Ezra reads from the Law of Moses from morning until midday, with priests scattered throughout the crowd to help them understand the meaning of what is being read. For many in the crowd, perhaps even most, they are hearing the Word of God and having it explained for the first time in their lives. The people's response to the Word is remarkable. They are so struck by the Lord's goodness and glory, while at the same time being deeply grieved by their own faithlessness, that the leaders have to urge them to enter the celebration: "'This day is holy to the LORD your God; do not mourn or weep.' For all the people wept when they heard the words of the law" (Neh 8:9). Almost overwhelmed by the deep conviction of their wandering into evil, they must be comforted

The Joy of Agreeing with God: Confession

by God's grace towards them. Along with grief over their sin, their immediate response is to worship by remembrance. Having heard in Deuteronomy that the day had come to celebrate Israel's time in the desert of Sinai, they come together the next day to begin the seven-day national campout, the Feast of Booths.

At the conclusion of the Feast of Booths, Nehemiah's account demonstrates God's purposes in awakening people to Truth and our relationship to it. God brings conviction in order to heal, and such healing brings joy. God is at work to reawaken his family in the assurance of being his family, to bring them back to know themselves as his beloved—for their good. When conviction comes, there are two necessary responses, both illustrated by the text: confession and renewal.

Two weeks after the Feast of Booths, the people again assemble "with fasting and in sackcloth, and with earth upon their heads," for the express purpose of making a united confession. After hearing the Law being read for three hours, they take the next three hours to confess their own sins and the iniquities of their fathers and to worship the Lord. We are given a condensed form of their confession, which demonstrates how clearly they have understood the import of God's Word.

First, they acknowledge who God is. True confession has to begin with God—with who he is as the foundational reality for everyone and everything dependent on him. These confessors agree that what he has said about himself is the truth. The confession begins,

> Stand up and bless the LORD your God from everlasting to everlasting. Blessed be your glorious name, which is exalted above all blessing and praise. "You are the LORD, you alone. You have made heaven, the heaven of heavens, with all their host, the earth and all that is on it, the seas and all that is in them; and you preserve all of them; and the host of heaven worships you. You are the LORD, the God who chose Abram and brought him out of Ur of the Chaldeans and gave him the name Abraham. You found his heart faithful before you, and made with him the covenant to give to his offspring the land of the Canaanite, the Hittite, the Amorite, the Perizzite, the Jebusite, and

> the Girgashite. And you have kept your promise, for you are righteous. (9: 5–8)

They make no speculation nor entertain anthropomorphic fantasies: no casting a god according to their own imaginations. Their confession of who God is comes from the very Word he has given. We can see they have truly received the Word that was read because they base their confession on it. In other words, they begin by saying, You are who you say you are, and everything else that matters flows from you, creator and owner of everything.

Second, their confession moves to an acknowledgement that God has acted consistently with who he is. They recount his acts of favor, mercy, and grace in the face of their own continuous rebellions. Their account of his way with them is punctuated by connections between God's character and his acts. In verse 17, "you are a God ready to forgive, gracious and merciful, slow to anger and abounding in steadfast love, and [you] did not forsake them." Though the people turned against God and embraced a golden calf, in great mercy he did not forsake them; instead of forsaking, "You gave your good Spirit to instruct them and did not withhold your manna from their mouth and gave them water for their thirst" (Neh 9:18–20). The people openly acknowledge that though time and again they rebelled and seemed to crave their own destruction, God continued to love his people and bring them deliverance and healing. They recall that "in the time of their suffering, they cried out to you and you heard them from heaven, and according to your great mercies you gave them saviors who saved them from the hand of their enemies" (Neh 9:27). So their common confession is clear that God is entirely in the right, and he has been merciful according to his character.

They agree with King David's model of confession in Psalm 51: "Against you, you only, have I sinned and done what is evil in your sight, so that you may be justified in your words and blameless in your judgment" (Ps 51:4). There is something like a personal abandonment to truth that lies at the heart of confession, and such an utterly vulnerable heart cannot come without being preceded by conviction. There is no getting around the truth: God

The Joy of Agreeing with God: Confession

is righteous, and we have done wrong and acted wickedly. We can see that they make no attempt to blame God or justify their own part. They make no attempt to excuse sin or rationalize their actions. Such total acceptance of responsibility is the opposite of our tendency to blame one's upbringing, one's psychology, one's enemies, or one's circumstances.

Abandoning self-protection, they recount the many and various ways that they as a people have rebelled against God. They own it completely. In particular, they acknowledge that the position they find themselves in, the circumstances of their last 150 years, is the result of their sin. They use the words of Scripture to describe what has come upon them. Summing up their acknowledgement of sin, they say, "Now, therefore, our God, the great, the mighty, and the awesome God, who keeps covenant and steadfast love, let not all the hardship seem little to you that has come upon us, upon our kings, our princes, our priests, our prophets, our fathers, and all your people, since the time of the kings of Assyria until this day. Yet you have been righteous in all that has come upon us, for you have dealt faithfully and we have acted wickedly" (Neh 9:32–33). Because conviction of sin is accompanied by the comforting truth that God forgives, God's people receive the freedom to confess fully and completely.

Accepting that God sees all, knows all, and still loves them, they have no need to hedge. Hedging, or partially excusing one's actions, results when we doubt God's goodness. When part of us does not accept that God is merciful and steadfast in his love, we will try to hide parts of our sin, diminish its severity, or convince ourselves that the sin is not really offensive to God. We will compose a story of the sin that puts it into a gray half-light, rather than belonging to darkness or light, death or life. It was not a theft, for example; it was borrowing with every intent to return, but somehow lacking the means to carry out the intention. On the other side, we sometimes accept Satan's account that denies the love and mercy of God, so that we recognize sin but will not confess because we are certain of condemnation. Yes, we say to ourselves, God sees our sin, and as he hates sin he must also hate us. Such a story denies the gospel—that God so loved the world that he came to die for us in our sin. It also denies God's power over our sin, as if our evil actions have the last word rather than the God who made and owns all. But when we abandon our own accounts and self-protecting stories to the merciful Lord and accept his account of things, like these returned exiles, our confession flows freely.

Most essentially, we see in the confession of the returned exiles that they accept God's account of their true identity and seek its restoration. This fundamental realignment with the Word of God is crucial for a people who has forgotten themselves. Through the Word, they rediscover what it means to be the people of God. Through the Word, they find their bearings. They find their name and what their name means: they are the people God chose, to whom he gave his name, and with whom he covenanted to dwell. They have wakened from a long, dark sleep full of dark dreams. In their confession, they accept that they are not like all the peoples of the earth, nor are they Jews because they have the same blood. Their identity is the covenant people of God.

RENEWAL

Because of their confession, they can heal. Conviction brings confession and renewal. At the conclusion of their long and thorough confession, the people say, "Because of all this, we make a firm covenant in writing; on the sealed document are the names of our princes, our Levites, and our priests" (Neh 9:38). Immediately following, chapter 10 begins with these names and then records the renewal of their covenant with God. We see that a response to conviction is not complete until you seek the restoration of right relationship with God. Having confessed that you have lived *outside* it in some way, renewing covenant is an expressed intention to live *within* it.

The whole people "enters into a curse and an oath to walk in God's Law that was given by Moses the servant of God, and to observe and do all the commandments of the LORD our Lord and his rules and his statutes" (Neh 10:29). The heart of this unfolding

The Joy of Agreeing with God: Confession

covenant is a reaffirmation of the very covenant that had been broken for generations and generations. They don't attempt a renegotiation along lines that will be more comfortable with their preferences. They commit to fulfill all the obligations God had required because they have come to accept that life with God means living the way he has said will be good. The people want that good life, but as their confession shows, the thing they want most of all is to please their Lord.

After their extensive confession and renewal of the covenant, they make a sign of this blessed relationship with God, their Protector. They dedicate the wall. The wall's completion had brought them together for the reading of the Law, and they recognized that God had given them a sign of restoration. With the dedication of wall, they are able to see a visible sign that their sins were forgiven and their covenant relationship had been restored. The outflow was joy: "And they offered great sacrifices that day and rejoiced, for God had made them rejoice with great joy; the women and children also rejoiced. And the joy of Jerusalem was heard far away" (Neh 12:43). God had brought them back and had received their penitence. Now he had set things right, and they had no doubt of it. How could they not rejoice?

CONFESSION AND THE EAST AFRICAN REVIVAL

Nowhere in recent history has this biblical pattern of confession and renewal been more evident or had wider waves of influence than the East African Revival, what we in East Africa sometimes call the movement of the Balokole (or The Saved People). Begun through the work of the Holy Spirit in the hearts of two Ugandan brothers, Simeon Nsibambi and Blasio Kigozi, the revival began in the late 1920s as essentially the gospel proclamation of freedom from sin at the personal cost of "walking in the light" (1 John). At the beginning, this proclamation was given to professing Christians in the Church of Uganda. As the brothers emphasized in their preaching, there could be no victory over sin in one's life, and

Part II: Paths to Rediscovering Joy

no sense of joy, unless sins were taken seriously and renounced on the basis of the cleansing blood of Jesus. The circle of influence broadened in 1929, when the English missionary doctor Joe Church visited Uganda for retreat from his work in Gahini, Rwanda. Meeting with Nsibambi for prayer and Bible reading, the two were filled with joy as they confessed sin to one another, crossing the racial boundary for intimate sharing that had hitherto been rarely approached. When Joe Church returned to Gahini, he was joined by other Ugandan faithful including the medical assistant Yosiya Kinuka (who is my wife's grandfather), and for the next several years the first phase of the East African Revival began to spread from Gahini mission hospital. But in 1935, Joe Church and Kinuka led a team from Gahini to the Church Missionary Society convention at Kabale, Uganda, where they joined Nsibambi and Kigozi along with contingents from across Uganda to report on the work of the Spirit in their local mission. It was there that the work of the Spirit set a particular stamp on the movement, scattering the participants with a distinct message and call to action that gave the legacy of the East African Revival.

Very similar to God's work among Israel recorded by Nehemiah, his movement at the Kabale Convention began with Bible reading and preaching that included both the seriousness of sin and the goodness of God to bleed on our behalf. As people of traditional African society, everyone there had killed animals and understood the meaning of blood as life, which is often lost on modern Americans. To speak of the blood of Jesus was a shorthand way of referring to atonement, a recognition that sin is so serious that a divine man was required to die in place of humanity in order to carry away our offense; the life of God was necessary to reconcile with God. The people gathered at the convention were struck with astonishment at the kindness of God to suffer for his offenders, and the personal nature of both offense and forgiveness swept the gathering. There seemed to be only one appropriate response: brokenness. Throughout the years of the revival, people reported a similar remarkable quality of this brokenness: they were simultaneously aware of the greatness of their sin and the love of

The Joy of Agreeing with God: Confession

God for them. They were convicted but not condemned; they were guilty but the door of their prison was open.

Whenever the Spirit brought this conviction, men and women felt an irresistible desire to bring their sin into the light. Following the message that Nsibambi, Kigozi, Church, and Kinuka had been preaching, the people were eager to publicly admit how they had lived hypocritically, had lied, stolen, or committed sexual sin. So there in the midst of the public gathering, people stood forward and spoke to the whole group about what they done and how much they were grieved by it. In token of their genuineness, their keenest aim was to make it right. Those confessing sin went immediately to those they had offended—whether present or absent—and asked forgiveness, offering restitution if it were possible. Typically, the move to admit wrong and seek forgiveness—so counter-intuitive in the traditional honor and shame society—resulted in a cascading effect. It was as if a convicted person was flooded with light and then brought that light with him or her when they came to confess. There in the places of worship, whether at the convention or in thousands of gatherings afterward, being truthful about sin and the need for God's forgiveness brought the whole group into the light of God. Finally, there was truth about who God is, who we are, and our relationship to him; it was right relationship restored, and the result was unbridled joy.

When the participants left the Kabale Convention of 1935, they took this experience and the light of truth with them. Returning to people to whom they needed to confess, they brought the idea of walking in the light to their villages and towns. Everywhere they went, revival broke out following the same pattern of proclamation, invitation to confess, and immediate response as the Holy Spirit brought conviction. And everywhere they went, the joy of renewed relationship with God was powerfully evident. They had to declare it and had to sing about it. The Balokole became known as singing people not only for their constant song of "Tukutendereza Yesu" ("We Praise You Jesus") but for many hymns and gospel songs of salvation. For decades, coming in waves, the churches of Rwanda, Uganda, Burundi, Kenya, and bordering nations experienced the influence of the East African Revival through its emphases on the seriousness of sin, the atoning blood of Jesus, the importance of confession, and the power of the Spirit to bring reconciliation.

Just as God knew Israel would be taken into exile and gave them prophecies of hope, God knew that East Africa would experience decades of strife and violence, from the oppression of General Idi Amin in Uganda to the civil wars of Rwanda, Burundi, and Kenya. Before these disasters of sin, he gave the message of walking in the light to create a people to bear witness to his love through the difficult times, and on the other side of them, to have a message of reconciliation to offer to divided societies. The message of the East African Revival—with acknowledgement of sin, forgiveness through the blood of Jesus, and the possibility of reconciliation—gives hope for societies torn by unthinkable evil. Without confession and the renewal of relationship with God that flows from it, there could be nothing like the joy that fills the churches of East Africa.

Accepting God's account of who we are and what is good for us, covenant renewal is a declaration to live accordingly. This agreement is what we enact in the Eucharist or Holy Communion. By his Word and Spirit, God has proclaimed that all who look to Jesus and trust that he forgives sin are participating in his kingdom. Baptism is the outward sign of belonging to that kingdom and family. When we come to the Table, we simultaneously accept God's account of our forgiveness through the Cross and our belonging to his kingdom, as well as declare our commitment to live accordingly. We say, "We offer you ourselves, our souls and bodies, to be a living sacrifice." We declare our desire to live according to God's rule, God's ways, as revealed in God's word. People who have been alienated from each other, even whole groups of people—tribes and nations—can experience the joy of renewed covenant with God by coming to the Table of the Lord together.

This order—from confession to restoration and renewal—purposely gives shape to the liturgy of the church in worship. Having heard the Word declared through preaching, if we find that we

The Joy of Agreeing with God: Confession

do not desire to live according to the Word, we should not come to the Table. Coming to the Table does not mean we have managed to avoid sinning; rather, coming to the Table means we want to be faithful and we need help. Flowing out of the Word preached, the Table celebration visibly declares the Gospel, and it is also our common confession of the gospel: God is holy; we have sinned; we need the blood of the Cross that offers forgiveness.

Subjectively, we often ought to feel joy when we participate in Communion. If we have understood the gospel we are jointly declaring, and have accepted our place in that story as mercifully forgiven and restored to fellowship with our King, then our renewed commitment to live by him, and with him, and in him is a taste of the renewed life. Standing in common devotion with others likewise being restored, under the rule of God and focused on his goodness, we find ourselves in the Garden remade.

QUESTIONS FOR REFLECTION

Is there a wrong thought or behavior in your life that you know needs to be confronted? What keeps you from bringing it to the light?

Try turning to one of the model prayers in Scripture (Moses in Exodus 33:12–23; Daniel's prayer in Daniel 9:3–19; or Nehemiah 1:4–11). Follow the model and let the Holy Spirit guide you into agreeing with God about your sin.

Consider times in your past when you felt conviction of sin and acted quickly to confess it. What were the outcomes?

9

The Joy of Fellowship

WHENEVER WESTERN PEOPLE VISIT churches in Rwanda, they almost always comment on how much joy we have and how loving of a welcome they receive. I (Cedric) used to think they were just being kind and saying what they thought was polite when visiting. Then after some years I finally visited the United States and came to understand what lay behind their statements: open and expressed joy has almost no place in Western life, even in services of worship. I kept urging my friends that they ought to incorporate dance! I was thinking maybe they just need to let it out bodily. But after visiting around the country and seeing the same thing over and over in different denominations, I realized that there's more going on than a difference in cultural or ethnic temperament. There is actually a lack of joy, and you cannot openly express what you do not have. In many ways, those experiences were the genesis of this book.

Just like Cedric noted, I (Ben) can never forget the first time I visited a rural village parish in Rwanda. Seventy-five years before, this parish had come into existence when a pair of preachers left the early center of the East African Revival at Gahini Hospital and came to the northern part of the country. Over a few days, as the preachers gave testimony to how God had broken the power of sin in their lives and brought them into his light, the village almost entirely had accepted the forgiveness offered by Jesus Christ, and the joy of their salvation had flooded from that village throughout the region. Though it was over seven decades later when I visited, they continued to use the call to worship begun during the revival. As I approached the parish and rounded a hilltop, I first caught the sound of a heavy beat on a massive calfskin drum, and then voices in song came to my ears, soon joined by the snap of clapping hands. My first glimpse as the church came into view was of a long line of dancing men, women, and children, leaping with arms held high. I didn't make it to the welcoming line before an old woman ran out to meet me, clutching me in a powerful embrace and rocking me left and right. I learned later that she had been a child when the Revival came and could remember the first laying of mud bricks for the church. She carried the joy of a revived life and in that moment offered one of its fruits: the joy of fellowship.

One of the issues addressed during the Revival was the wounding and sin occasioned by colonialism, especially how it had leeched into the church. Although early secretaries of the Church Missionary Society, especially under the leadership of Henry Venn, had been committed to the Pauline principles of establishing self-governing, self-propagating, and self-supporting churches, the later nineteenth and early twentieth century reversed policy and largely took on colonial attitudes of paternalism. The senior leadership of both the Ugandan Church and Rwandan Mission was entirely white, and there was a stark divide between Africans and Europeans throughout the church. As indicated in our chapter on Confession, the Revival brought together both Africans and whites, and the Holy Spirit left no sin unexposed; God confronted the pride and arrogance of the Europeans and the bitterness and resentment of Africans. In confessing sin, each group found freedom to acknowledge their part, and as they offered forgiveness, the Spirit healed their wounds and gave them unity and love. They discovered reconciliation and fellowship in the Holy Spirit, along with a unique facet of God's joy.

Part II: Paths to Rediscovering Joy

For both of us, God has brought us into an intimate fellowship in the Spirit across ethnic and cultural boundaries that we had never even considered as something to pursue. The idea of heart-level closeness with someone from a radically different culture was never offered to either of us in the communities where we grew up, and if anything, the possibility of it was denied. But God has woven our lives together. Our children know we are one family, and whether we are together or apart, we experience the joy of fellowship as we support each other, teach each other, and share in sufferings.

The joy of fellowship that we experience together is also part of God's design for life within his local church. As we understand from the New Testament epistles, members of a local church are part of a "family"—the favorite metaphor of the early church for their holy society. There is a spiritual reality that they have one God and Father, that the same Holy Spirit binds them all together, that whether or not they like each others' personalities, they are people of one blood: brothers and sisters through the blood of Jesus. When these realities of oneness, unity, and familial interdependency are not quenched by strife but are allowed to flourish and give strength, the local family of Christ experiences the feelings of God for his beloved. The joy of fellowship is nothing less than a taste of God's own love within the fellowship of Father, Son, and Holy Spirit.

SECURE MUTUAL SUPPORT

As Jesus prepared his disciples for his death, departure, and their new season of life dependent on the Spirit, he was honest that "in the world you will have trouble" (John 16:33), and "if they have persecuted me, they will also persecute you" (John 15:20). Even so, he encouraged them that he would not leave them alone but would send the Spirit to comfort, counsel, and guide. Along with the gift of the Spirit, he also gave them the gift of each other.

He framed the whole conversation about his departure with the action of washing their feet and the command to "love one another: just as I have loved you, you also are to love one another.

By this all people will know that you are my disciples, if you have love for one another" (John 13:34–35). The way that these disciples would hold together and show that they were still connected to Jesus is that they would have love for each other. At the end of that long evening of the Last Supper, Jesus prayed for them. He concluded his prayer and John concludes his account of the upper room with this: "I do not ask for these only, but also for those who will believe in me through their word, that they may all be one, just as you, Father, are in me, and I in you, that they also may be in us, so that the world may believe that you have sent me. The glory that you have given me I have given to them, that they may be one even as we are one, I in them and you in me, that they may become perfectly one, so that the world may know that you sent me and loved them even as you loved me.... I made known to them your name, and I will continue to make it known, that the love with which you have loved me may be in them, and I in them" (John 17:20–26).

Jesus leaves them with no uncertainty that their unity with each other is inseparably connected with the Spirit he is sending, and that when they are being obedient to the Spirit, they will experience love for each other. The love they will have will come by the Spirit from the Father. It will be the same kind of love that exists between the Father, Son, and Spirit, bringing with it a host of blessings and gifts. Together, they will be reflecting their design as God's image-bearers. As we have established from the first chapter of this work, the subjective feeling of rightness with God and his life in us is joy. When the community of Jesus acts in the love of God in the unity of the Spirit, they will be filled with a sense of joy in their fellowship, in their oneness.

In the course of life together, this joy can take us by surprise, whenever we lean in to one another for support. As Jesus's high priestly prayer indicates, the blessings he prays for are derived from acts of love, from those moments when weakness in one is met by strength in another, or need in one is met by resource from another. Mutual service calls attention to a shared life and love.

One reason we think the local churches of Africa (and the developing world generally) experience more joy of fellowship is

Part II: Paths to Rediscovering Joy

that developing societies present far more opportunities for mutual support and service. When the necessities of life are more obviously dependent on rain coming in a timely way and quantity, when the whims of government may leave parts of society suddenly vulnerable, when swarms of locust may decimate a whole season of crops, or invading tribal militias may deprive of life and property, we have regular reminders that we need each other. There has not been a generation in Rwanda untouched by a sense of life's vulnerability. In village life, we suffer together but also endure and survive together. If a family has no food, they go to their fellow church member or to the Pastor. And when the Pastor has nothing to give, he will find church members who have something to help the family. The burden for one becomes the burden for the entire church so that no one will suffer alone. From very long distances, traveling over hard mountains and sometimes barefoot, even having little to eat of their own, brothers and sisters want to bear their part of the church's burden. For funerals, baptisms, weddings and other functions, everyone around wants to take a share in preparing the activities because it is a matter for the entire community, whether of celebration or sorrow. When the challenges come, if the local church does not cling to each other, there is nowhere else to look for material support. In these critical circumstances, every little sacrifice speaks the love of God, and the fruit of that enacted love is joy.

During the recent food shortages brought on by coronavirus quarantines and subsequent heavy rains, pastors were among the most vulnerable people in the country. The churches were closed, and pastors live on tithes. Although the government gave food aid across the country, they left out church workers and clergy. But God used even this to demonstrate the power of his love. In many cases, pastors still sought out widows and vulnerable families in order to share what little they had. These sacrifices tangibly declare an other-worldly love that has bound God's people together in a family. Many Muslims have taken note during this season and have become open to the gospel because they see this love is more than just words. Over the course of a week, four different sheikhs asked to talk to me (Cedric) about what they were seeing. Through sharing and sacrifice, and through witness to God's love, joy has been multiplied.

For Christians in the West, material prosperity gives with one hand but takes away with the other. The incredible standard of living and layers of social safety nets have sheltered Christians from the physical vulnerability faced by much of the world. Yes, there are many American families who struggle with food insecurity, but social programs prevent the kind of devastation of extreme poverty common in the global south. When is the last time you heard of an American starving to death? But the cost of material prosperity and security is a loss of mutual support and interdependence. Added to that is a heritage of independence and cultural attitude of self-sufficiency, with the toxic result that pride prevents many people from making their needs known. Or worse, when needs are known, some look with scorn on the vulnerable or blame them for their weakness. While social programs protect thousands from dangerous situations, the programs remove the necessity of the church to "carry one another's burdens." One of the almost unnoticed casualties is the loss of joy through sharing burdens.

In places of material prosperity, it is important to remember there are other kinds of burdens and other kinds of poverty. Jayakumar Christian, a leader of World Vision in India, has written persuasively in *God of the Empty-Handed* about the need for Christians to reconsider poverty more holistically, recognizing that impoverishment has many dimensions. If value is defined by the wealth of God's kingdom, then there must surely be moral and spiritual impoverishment that is as devastating as physical poverty. The truly wealthy may well be those who have far fewer material resources in this world.

If Western Christians are to rediscover joy, they will have to contend with this notion. Taking this spiritual reality into account, we find that wherever we live we are daily rubbing shoulders with impoverished people in desperate need of support and someone to share their burdens. We all have burdens to carry that we cannot carry on our own, from unresolved conflicts with parents to the pains of handling traumatic experiences. God never designed a completely self-sufficient man. Rather, as the Kenyan liturgy declares, "I am because we are, and we are because he is." The Church consists of people who need others to fully live God's design and to discover what it is like to live with others in their identity as new creations in Christ. We are made in such a way that our most essential needs—for life, love, and significance—are met only in the fellowship of the redeemed. When we accept the spiritual need for others to remind us of our identity (Col 3:15–17), hear our confessions and come together to God for healing (Jas 5:13–16), speak words of encouragement (1Thess 5:11), and show us how to walk the way of Christ (1 Cor 11:1), then we will be doing the necessary work of sharing out the weight of spiritual burdens. As anyone can see, this mutual support and interdependence requires humility. Only those churches that practice humility will have access to the joy of fellowship. There is no other way to it.

LEARNING FROM ONE ANOTHER

Among the greatest teachers we were given are the people with whom we share life. In every place where his church is gathered, God has given all the truth and wisdom necessary for that people to flourish and grow. Those who have walked life's journey longer have seen situations and phases of life that the younger have yet to pass. Likewise, in whatever trouble we find ourselves, whether a circumstance, ethical quandary, or intellectual puzzle, someone else has been here before us. And in God's perfect economy, he distributes wisdom, gifts, and experiences so that they can be shared through the local body of Christ and beyond.

In the first few years after I (Cedric) had yielded to Jesus as Lord and turned from Islam, I was desperate to understand how to negotiate the complex relationships I now had. My father was a sheikh trying to kill me, but the Christians were often afraid of me as a former imam and Islamic apologist, not unlike what the apostle Paul initially felt from the church in Jerusalem. I was filled with boldness for Christ, but I struggled to find close, intimate connection or a guide to help me through these challenges. During that time of loneliness, I met a former sheikh named Salim who was then a pastor in one of the biggest Pentecostal churches in Rwanda. He told me what he had passed through when he had turned from Islam to Jesus, and we talked often about the different assumptions and reasoning between Islam and Christianity. In particular, he helped me understand what I was experiencing as I read the Bible with the help of the Holy Spirit—a completely foreign concept to Muslims. Through him and the work of the Spirit, I shifted from understanding the world through Islamic teaching to aligning with the new faith that I had found in Jesus. His counsel played a big role in the next stages of my growth, as iron sharpens iron and so a brother sharpens another (Prov 27:17). I often received not only encouragement and counsel, but also rebuke and correction towards sound doctrine. Only one who had come from Islam to know Jesus could have understood both what I needed to learn and what I needed to avoid. For me, not only did I receive the joy of coming to right understanding, but also the joy of walking the journey with a brother who cared. While I had thought no one could sympathize with my story, God knew my need and sent me a teacher; I received the knowledge and care I needed, but I also got the unexpected gift of joy in fellowship.

The story of Apollos can give us a hint of another facet to this joy. In Acts 18:24 and following, Apollos came to Ephesus shortly after Paul had left his friends Priscilla and Aquila there. A Jewish native of Alexandria, he "was a learned man, with a thorough knowledge of the Scriptures. He had been instructed in the way of the Lord, and he spoke with great fervor and taught about Jesus accurately, though he knew only the baptism of John. He began to speak boldly in the synagogue. When Priscilla and Aquila heard him, they invited him to their home and explained to him the way of God more adequately." It is clear that Apollos had believed in Jesus but rushed to preach while he still had some important things to understand. He had gifts and the message, but his message was distorted because he preached the baptism of John rather than the adoption of God into the name and family of Jesus. He had the zeal, he had the gifts, but his understanding

Part II: Paths to Rediscovering Joy

of Jesus's redemptive work and mission was incomplete. Apollos needed someone who understood well and had experience to help him into a more sound doctrine. Priscilla and Aquila were in that position. They had become disciples at Corinth as Paul lived with them and taught the gospel for a year and a half. No doubt they listened attentively as he engaged others' questions, watching his debates and having opportunity to follow up in private with their own questions. Because of this opportunity for deep teaching, they were able to help Apollos grasp the gospel fully so that his next ministry to Corinth was a blessing. In both cases of learning and sharing the truth, all of them received the joy of knowing more and growing to understand more of the Lord Jesus through fellowship. Such fellowship required great humility.

For Apollos, he had to humble himself to acknowledge that the uneducated tentmakers had a more comprehensive understanding of God's truth. God enabled him to see that despite all his learning and thorough knowledge, he was missing some things that this couple had. On the other side, Priscilla and Aquilla took a risk to approach the brilliant itinerant philosopher with his big vocabulary and sophisticated reasoning. They risked embarrassment, rejection, and possibly ridicule. Anyone who has contradicted a professor's bold assertions knows that it was undoubtedly humbling for the couple to suggest that they might have knowledge he lacks. But all of them were committed to truth, and through their mutual humility they were able to learn together. They found the truth that they were part of the same fellowship in Jesus. Their fellowship in the Spirit produced a powerful stimulus for the upbuilding of the church in Ephesus and then Corinth. It must have been an enriching and encouraging time, full of the blessing of joy, because it changed them all.

Their experience of fellowship emboldened all of them, so that we later read of Apollos as a significant teacher of the Church, while the couple becomes the cornerstone of several successive churches in their home and is listed foremost in Paul's greetings to the Roman church as "my fellow workers in Christ Jesus, who risked their necks for my life, to whom not only I give thanks but all the churches of the Gentiles give thanks as well" (Rom 3–4). Joy and the pleasure of service had become fuel for them, so that they were willing to give all for the sake of the gospel.

As we see in the case of Aquilla and Priscilla, this joy of fellowship can be just the thing that propels timid Christians into boldness. It can be like a switch that turns a worldly inclined Christian into one willing to live fully for Jesus. Such a person finds that the joy of fellowship in the Spirit—of learning together, of being known and loved, of having gifts and a voice that matters eternally—is better than any fleeting pleasure the world can offer. But as we see with Apollos and friends, the joy of fellowship requires vulnerability, risk, and humility.

FELLOWSHIP IN MISSION

On the surface, the apostle Paul had very little in common with the Christian community of Philippi. A Jew born in Tarsus of Cilicia, Paul had spent his youth learning from the rabbi Gamaliel in Jerusalem, becoming steeped in the Law and the Prophets. By all accounts he was zealous for the Law and for the people of Israel, willing to persecute and see Christians executed until he encountered the glorified Lord Jesus. Until he came to Philippi, his preaching and ministry always began with the Law and the Prophets, from which he reasoned with Jews and God-fearing gentiles first in the synagogue and then in spaces outside it. At the Roman colony of Philippi, there was no synagogue, and although there was a place of prayer by the river where "some women" including Lydia came to worship, none were called Jews but only "worshiper[s] of God." Paul and his companions stayed in Philippi, and the church that took root from Lydia's house came to include a formerly demon-possessed girl who prophesied for the god Apollo, and a jailer with his entire household. We know little else about the composition of the church except that it grew as an entirely gentile church. Those who responded to the gospel in Philippi had cultural and religious backgrounds far from their apostle. They had grown up with a Greco-Roman pantheon, along

Part II: Paths to Rediscovering Joy

with the worship of the colony's patron Octavius Caesar Augustus. They had consulted spirits and oracles—one of them had been a medium—and had been devoted to the values of the principalities and powers. At this period, there were about 10,000 people living in Philippi, comprised of an Italian privileged class, native Macedonian laborers, and an immigrant merchant class. The forty percent of the population who were Italians were Roman citizens by birth, many of whom were retired centurions who had been given land and a pension. The sixty percent who were non-citizens were undoubtedly envious of the Italians' privileges. As we know from Paul's experiences in Philippi, Roman citizenship mattered there—a lot. As a Jew from the eastern provinces, the fact of Paul's Roman citizenship was such a surprise because he was so different from the Philippian Italians.

Despite their significant differences in background, custom, knowledge, and experiences, Paul and the Philippian Church developed a loving relationship. As evident in his letter, it was a connection replete with the bond of joy. Anyone who attends at all closely to Paul's letter to Philippi notices the fifteen times he speaks of joy or rejoicing, which is more than in any other book of the New Testament. Notwithstanding his circumstances—he was writing from imprisonment—Paul cannot help but express his joy when communicating with this beloved group of people because it is a special kind of joy that goes beyond circumstances, the joy of fellowship in God's mission.

The second chapter of the letter links an attitude with the kind of life that will yield joy for all. Paul's memorable urging in verse 2 frames the idea: "*Complete my joy* by being of the same mind, having the same love, being in full accord and of one disposition." After pointing to Jesus as the picture and source of this mind and posture, he encourages them towards this joy through three examples of people living God's mission: himself, Timothy, and Epaphroditus.

He begins with his own pleasure at being a living sacrifice: "Even if I am to be poured out as a libation upon the sacrificial offering of your faith, I am glad and rejoice with you all" (2:17).

The Joy of Fellowship

Whether he lives or dies in this imprisonment, he is full of joy because the Philippians are earnest in trusting Jesus. As he looks at them, the Spirit shouts inwardly, bringing the joy of the Lord. The Spirit says to Paul: "See my work through you!" In the next verse, he highlights the fellowship that they share in this joy: "Likewise, you also should be glad and rejoice with me." Very often, the mechanism God uses to draw us into his joy is sharing the news of God's work with brothers and sisters. As Paul rejoices in the Spirit about the faithfulness of the Philippians, he draws them into the joy of the Spirit. Even for just a moment, through Paul's eyes and by means of his words, they can see themselves the way God sees them. He pulls them away from the challenges of their circumstances and into the reckonings and measuring of God. The Lord's reference points are very different from ours, so when we walk around in his landscape for a bit, everything looks different than we saw it a moment before.

Then Paul points to Timothy and Epaphroditus. Timothy is a living example of the attitude he presented earlier in the chapter. "Do nothing from selfishness or conceit, but in humility count others better than yourselves. Let each of you look not only to his own interests, but also to the interests of others" (2:3–4), and then, "Do all things without grumbling or questioning that you may be blameless and innocent" (2:14–15). He then presents Timothy: "I have no one like him, who will be genuinely anxious for your welfare. They all look after their own interests, not those of Jesus Christ. But Timothy's worth you know" (2:20–22). Timothy is living the mind of Christ. It is as if Paul says, I'm sending you an example of what I'm talking about. And as Paul does so, he rejoices. In 3 John, John says, "Nothing gives me greater joy than to hear that my children are walking in the truth" (v 4). Likewise, to the Philippians Paul has said that his joy is complete when his children have the mind of Christ. That he can send Timothy, with full confidence in his self-forgetful, Jesus-honoring life, he takes joy. Every pastor will say the same. Nothing gives us greater joy than to see brothers and sisters becoming self-forgetful and making decisions

PART II: PATHS TO REDISCOVERING JOY

to honor Jesus because they have been letting the Word change them.

Finally, Paul honors the Philippian messenger Epaphroditus, calling him "my brother and fellow worker and fellow soldier" (2:25). He has shown his faith. He has lived the Christlike mind, pouring out his life as a sacrificial offering. In order to bring aid to Paul in his imprisonment, he had traveled hundreds of miles and endured hardship to support God's mission through Paul. Serving in this perilous way, he had suffered illness and nearly died. Paul uses this selfless commitment to God's mission as another model for the orientation of life that brings joy. He can say, "rejoice at seeing him again" and "receive him in the Lord with all joy; and honor such men, for he nearly died for the work of Christ" (2:29–30). The rejoicing and the honor are linked to his service in the work of Christ.

Joy is given by the Spirit; it comes from God. It is the note of his heart. When we feel it, we feel ourselves in rhythm with his pleasure. What gives God pleasure is when we think and live and act in accordance with what he values. It is a further gift that our brothers and sisters in Christ can reveal God's pleasure to us, so that we can draw each other into joy and rejoicing, just like Paul did with the Philippians. By taking a moment, reorienting according to the Lord's kingdom, and celebrating what he has done and is doing, we can participate in the Spirit's joy together.

I (Ben) have learned this most acutely through my relationship with Rwandan friends. We come from vastly different cultures, with contrasting norms and customs, but that very difference provides a kind of kingdom mirror that clarifies those things in my life that are truly part of the kingdom rather than compromises with my culture. The essential ways of God are supra-cultural, resonating in the hearts of believers of every background. Although we might not understand the nuances of another culture, the Spirit in us says "Amen" to what glorifies God. Through my friends' eyes and their sensitivity to the Holy Spirit, I can see where I have been deviating from the honor of Jesus but also see what is pleasing him.

Finally, like Paul and the Philippians, our shared commitment to the cause of Jesus brings constant reason for joy. As we communicate weekly, we rejoice together at our sufferings for Christ and the victories we each get to witness. Living in the United States, which has been hard ground for gospel seed for several decades now, I have treasured participation in the fertile spreading of seed across East Africa. When Cedric preaches to thousands in South Sudan, Zambia, Uganda, or Rwanda, I and my congregation rejoice at the privilege of praying. When we receive testimonies from those who have turned to Jesus from native African religion or Islam, we praise God for his goodness. We also feel a sometimes overwhelming sense of joy and humility that we can be part of God's mission. Although we see few conversions in our own city and struggle against the thorns trying to choke out our gospel seed, we are encouraged because we have fellowship in the mission of God.

QUESTIONS FOR REFLECTION

Think about a few people on whom you depend for encouragement and support. How can you outwardly and enthusiastically let them know you value them? If you do, you will share joy.

In your church are there people who seem outside the recognizable social groups? How might you extend friendship or include them in your own circle of fellowship?

Rather than thinking about your own desire for friendship or companionship, how often do you follow the pattern of Christ and look for lonely people? Consider the gift of joy you can give.

10

The Path to Joy Includes Suffering

EVEN AS WE WRITE this book, we are both shut in our homes due to our governments' responses to the global coronavirus pandemic. Though the rates of infection have abated, we know other consequences of the response are still unfolding. Not only societies but also churches have been divided on what ought to have been done and what ought to guide plans and decisions going forward.

Like many others, my mind has sought points of comparison in the past. As a student and scholar of the Middle Ages, I (Ben) find myself considering the fourteenth century. Following major volcanic eruptions around 1300—likely in Mexico—a great volcanic dust cloud caused a drop in temperatures and crop failures across the northern hemisphere in the first decade of the century. Global weather patterns changed; in 1303, 1306, and 1307, the Baltic Sea completely froze over for the first time ever recorded. Talk about climate change! In 1315, heavy rains caused famine across Europe. But it was the mid-century that draws my attention.

In 1346 rumors reached Europe that a devasting plague had come from China, leaving whole regions of China and India depopulated.[1] Then in October of 1347, Genoese merchant ships

1. Barbara Tuchman's *A Distant Mirror* remains the most accessible

The Path to Joy Includes Suffering

drifted into the harbor of Messina, Sicily, flying the plague flag. Bearing a rich cargo from Caffa (now Feodosiya) on the coast of the Black Sea, the ships' cargo proved too tempting for the Sicilians. When they rowed out, they found dead and dying sailors with black, swollen glands the size of an egg in their armpits and groin, which oozed black blood and pus. These swellings, named buboes, gave the name to the bubonic plague, or Black Death. An even more virulent airborne form, named pneumonic plague, infected the lungs. While the bubonic strain spread by contact and pneumonic by droplets, the infectious period lasted for at least a week before symptoms showed.

The disease could be so lethal that a person might go to bed without symptoms and never wake up, although typically death came within three days of showing symptoms. The mortality rate of the overall population ranged widely, from about one fifth to upwards of ninety percent of the population in some places. The more densely populated sites, such as monasteries and urban centers, fared the worst. Paris lost half its population; Florence up to eighty percent; Venice, Hamburg, and Bremen around sixty percent. Some villages that were hit particularly hard simply disappeared. The brother of the Italian poet Petrarch was a Carthusian monk who buried every member of his monastery, sometimes three a day, until at last he was left alone with his dog.

Although admittedly speculative, historians estimate that between one third to one half the global population died of the fourteenth century pandemic. In Europe alone, this meant between 20 to 30 million. When one considers a major earthquake in 1348, as well as the Hundred Years' War, and the moral decline of the Roman Catholic Church, there seemed to be every reason to believe that the End of Days had come.

And yet, it was not the end. In fact, one of the major responses to the suffering of the fourteenth century was revival in personal piety. Not long after the plague, John Wycliffe in England began his project of translating the Bible into English so that common people could hear the Word in their own language and

---
account of the fourteenth-century plagues.

Part II: Paths to Rediscovering Joy

seek scriptural truth on their own. His efforts for the gospel won him the title the Evangelical Doctor. At the same time, manuals for private devotion proliferated and spread through the noble houses of Europe. In the soil of horrible misery and suffering, the Lord germinated seeds of righteousness and reform. Although almost everyone at the time accepted that God was judging his people for the moral decline of the Church, what they equally accepted was God's right over his world, to rule it as he saw fit. Interpretations and responses varied, but the Christian world knew it was part of God's plan. They accepted the sovereignty of God the Creator.

From Genesis 3, it is clear that the Fall resulted in human suffering. To some extent it is the common suffering of all creation. All of the prophets in the Old Testament were clear through their words and deeds that suffering is part of our lives. The Psalmist speaks with certainty: "the length of our days is seventy years or eighty years if we have the strength, yet their span is but troubles and sorrow, for they quickly pass and we fly away" (Ps 90:10). And Ecclesiastes reflects what everyone around the world knows, "for everything there is a season and a time for every matter under heaven: a time to be born and a time to die," and between birth and death a set of things both bad or good in their turns (Ecc 3:1–8). We would, of course, like to avoid suffering, and every creature—man and beast—prefers pleasure to pain. But if we pay any heed to Jesus's teaching and his mission, we cannot miss the key paradox of eternal life that ultimate life comes through death, and joy comes through suffering. It is the principle with which we began this exploration of joy: "for the joy set before him, he endured the cross, despising its shame" (Heb 12:2).

SUFFERING IS PART OF HIS PLAN.

Among all of Jesus's teachings to his disciples, the one they simply could not grasp was that the Son of Man came to die, to give his life as a ransom. No matter how many times he indicated his mission, with words like, "unless a kernel of wheat falls to the ground and dies, it remains only a single seed. But if it dies, it produces many seeds" (John 12:24), the meaning was hidden from them. And when finally he explicitly explained that he must suffer and be killed, the disciples were having none of it, leading to Jesus rebuking Peter (Matt 16:21–23). It made no sense to them that goodness and an everlasting kingdom could come out of misery and defeat. The king who would rule forever obviously could not die. Here on the other side of his resurrection, Christians know that his death was necessary.

The Almighty God had determined not to abandon and destroy his creation, but instead he desired to draw near and to renew mankind. To those embracing death, he would bring life. To those uncreating themselves, he would bring his Word that would recreate. But there had to be a death. The corruption in each and every human brought unravelling death into their lives, as well as punishment after death. How could the pervasive death from sin be dealt with so that man could be reconciled with God?

From his first movements towards fallen man, he taught the necessity of atonement. When God began the healing mission, he moved towards the family of Israel. Adopting them as his own family, he did the unimaginable: he came to dwell among them in the Tabernacle. But for the Holy One to be near such sinful brokenness, he established a pattern of annual atoning sacrifice that would allow him to dwell with them without consuming them by his holiness. On the day of atonement, the high priest would take two goats to the Tabernacle. One would be burnt on the altar as a sin offering. Over the other, the priest would confess the sins of the people, and bearing these sins, the goat would be taken to the wilderness. In one, the sin is consumed; in the other, the sin is sent away.

These two acts have a combined signification. In consuming the sacrifice and the sins for which it dies, God sends the sin of the people away from them, in order that he might remain with them. Rather than destroying them by his holy presence, his power is directed to atoning sacrifice. When God came near in his glory, when he came to receive the sin offering of the atoning sacrifice, the burning of the sacrifice signified that his holiness consumed and destroyed it. By destroying their sin, he could be with his people.

Part II: Paths to Rediscovering Joy

But as even perceptive Israelites understood, the blood of animals could not truly atone for the sins of a rational, rebellious man (Heb 10:3-4). God had given a system that would find its reality later.

When Jesus died that Friday, he walked fully into his role as the Lamb of God. When he came down the hill on the 10th of Abib to the shouts of Hosanna, he set his will to be the lamb for this people. Like the lamb chosen by each household in the Old Covenant, he was the lamb for the household of man. By obedience, Hebrews tells us, he became the perfect sacrifice. But how does this perfect sacrifice restore humankind? The answer is in what he suffered in his death.

In ancient Israel, on the Day of Atonement, God came near in glory. When Jesus the great high priest offered himself as a sacrifice for the sins of the world, God came near in glory. Stepping sinless to the Cross, Jesus wrapped the sin of the world about him. As the apostles write, "he bore our sins in his body on the tree" (1 Peter 2:24). Somewhere in the darkness of that death, those sins were consumed. Jesus endured judgment. Having died in the flesh, he went to the Second Death and walked through it. Bringing human nature with him, bound up in him and inseparable from him, Jesus came again into the glorious presence of God. And our God, who is a consuming fire, consumed the sin. Jesus alone could endure this death, this wrath, because of the divine life that was in him. Being the Word of God, life answered life, and in the unification of Father, Son, and Holy Spirit, along with human nature, a new human nature was revealed, shed of sin, corruption, and death.

It was crucial to his plan that he took our human nature with him, that he took our sin. It is crucial that it was dealt with, that it was consumed, because it is in this that he died the death we would otherwise die. Every person must die in the flesh, many will keep on dying; but because of Jesus, those who trust in him will not face a Second Death.

God has shown plainly that his plan to heal us had to be through suffering and death. Life comes from death. Jesus allows no compromise when he says, "If anyone would come after me, he must deny himself and take up his cross and follow me" (Luke 9:23).

When he says "he must deny himself," Jesus shows he knows our tendencies. We want to allow ourselves some other way to life. But the God who holds life and death declares that there is no other way.

Our acceptance of this truth and the sovereign authority of God to order the universe as pleases him is essential for finding joy. Admittedly, though, this move of faith is more difficult in the midst of pain and affliction. Whatever the source, we just want the pain to end. But if we have a life suffused with submission to God, thoroughly shaped by the gospel, when we find ourselves suffering we have a pattern for understanding our situation within the crucial story. The troubles of our circumstances are bound up with a fallen and perishing world, and they are confined to it. Whatever our trouble, it is implicated in Jesus's death and its spiritual consequences have been dealt with. This earthly suffering is limited and confined; it cannot follow us forever.

BEING PART OF THE PAINFUL PLAN

The Scriptures tell us that all of creation waits with longing for the joyous completion of the story, when all the pieces will fall into place and make sense. Like a woman in childbirth, as soon as she sees the baby, pain has its meaning fully explained and is deemed worthwhile. Imagine all the discomfort of pregnancy and the pain of delivery without knowing the reason. This is what Paul talks about as the creation waits eagerly because we know that one day the outworking of death will end. We have faith that our present sufferings are not worth comparing with the glory that will be revealed in us, when there will be no more hunger, poverty, sickness and pain (Rom 8:18).

When we accept the plan of God simply because it is part of his rule, joy rises in us mysteriously. We were designed for his rule, so our affirmation of its right execution becomes a point of alignment for our hearts. But like the disciples protesting Jesus's intentions, it is on this issue of the necessity of suffering that we tend to find ourselves most resistant to the ways of God's rule. It has often been said that every person wants to deny the need for a savior. No

Part II: Paths to Rediscovering Joy

one wants to admit we need saving. It is also true that we would like to deny the necessity of suffering and death to overturn the effects of the Fall. We have a problem with pain.

In his book titled *The Problem of Pain*, which addresses this subject, C.S. Lewis wrote, "Pain insists upon being attended to. God whispers to us in our pleasures, speaks in our consciences, but shouts in our pains. It is his megaphone to rouse a deaf world."[2] Our human weakness, cosmic fallenness, and need for God are always present, telling us that we need the forgiveness and power of Christ. But pleasure and busyness bring confusion and deafen us to it. Pain reminds us of the necessity of the atonement, and personal pain and suffering bring it home to us that we need atoning and transformation. The world needs renewal, and we need it too. Christian, even you, washed and sanctified, continue to need the love and power of God. You were saved by the gospel, but you also continue in need of the gospel.

In the midst of our afflictions, sometimes only the big picture of the gospel gives meaning to what we face. Mukagatashya Immaculee is a widow of the 1994 Genocide in Rwanda. I (Cedric) first learned about her while serving in Kivu Diocese in Gisenyi. I was visiting my friend, and he invited me to go along as he visited his friend. When we reached the house, we were met by a woman with a cheerful smile, who greeted me with a joyful, "Praise the Lord!" But having no arms or legs, she called from the floor where she was lying inside the house. Identified as Tutsis, her husband and her four children were murdered in the Genocide, but her suffering was worse than theirs. The human depravity was the worst that Satan could inspire. After she witnessed the murder of her family, their home was burnt to the ground. Then she was raped and left with HIV. Her legs and arms were cut off, and a tree branch was shoved into her vagina. The suffering of Job cannot stand beside what she endured. Although I have heard many accounts of atrocities, I could hardly bear her story.

What overwhelmed me and challenged me to give more praise to God is when she explained how she had discovered

2. Lewis, *The Problem*, 91.

The Path to Joy Includes Suffering

meaning for why she lives. Her reason was that many people are encouraged in their faith or towards faith in God by seeing her continue to have joy in life regardless of her endless pain. Satan and his captive slaves had caused it, but her suffering made sense to her as part of the gospel. In the fallen world where the enemy clings to destruction and seeks only to steal, kill, and destroy, the light of life will always be attacked. She came to understand herself as a living sign of God's salvation in this world. Satan did his worst, but she lives! Everlasting life awaits her, but for now she testifies to the love of God and how God's light can shine in the worst circumstances. Has she been cured from HIV? No. Were her legs and arms restored? No. Were her memories erased? No! But the power and grace of God are sufficient even for this. She told me herself!

It seems impossible that there can be joy through such suffering, but even that impossibility is part of the gospel message. Jesus did what no other could, and he gives what cannot be attained any other way. Jesus passed through the deepest depths and through the darkest valley of the shadow of death. And he came back, opening the way to everlasting life and bringing the joy of his Spirit and the eternal realms. People who have received his gift and are filled with the light of heaven can have peace and contentment in every condition. As Immaculee shows, and those sufferers of the fourteenth century demonstrated, when we see our circumstances as part of the Sovereign God's plans of redemption, we have a story of hope to tell. We carry it within us. Because it's the true story, when we tell it, the joy of the Lord can flow in.

QUESTIONS FOR REFLECTION

When you think about the sovereignty of God and his rule over everything, do you accept that he is not surprised by global pandemics and natural disasters? Why is such an acceptance crucial to having joy?

Why do you think people so strongly resist the idea that pain and suffering can have meaning?

Part II: Paths to Rediscovering Joy

Immaculee has found joy as a witness to Christ's power to overcome evil. Is there a part of your life that you could reimagine in this way, that although evil has done its work, yet you live in the light of God?

11

The Joy of Sharing in the Suffering of Christ

AS THE LAST CHAPTER showed, the joy of the Lord is available in the midst of any kind of suffering as a participation in the truth of the gospel. But there is also a unique joy that is only given through a certain kind of affliction: suffering for the sake of Christ's name. To such suffering Jesus calls us, and for it he has promised grace sufficient for it: "Remember what I told you: 'A servant is not greater than his master.' If they persecuted me, they will persecute you also" (John 15:20), but "be of good cheer! I have overcome the world" (John 16:33).

Some years ago when I (Cedric) was in class at Uganda Christian University with Rev. Abraham Ngor, who later became Bishop of Gogrial Diocese in South Sudan, he shared with me the need for the gospel in South Sudan and how people are suffering with hunger and poverty due to the never-ending civil wars in the newly formed state of South Sudan. As he was describing their plight, I felt the burden to encourage them with the love of Christ and to proclaim his sacrifice for them. Years later, the time became ripe. When I mentioned my desire and intention to venture on a mission in South Sudan, I encountered opposition, including from my wife Dorcus. They were worried based on radio and television

Part II: Paths to Rediscovering Joy

reports of Rwandan peace-keeping soldiers serving with the United Nations, who testified to the destabilization of the country and the prevalence of violence.

In my prayers, I kept feeling peace and joy about going to serve the people in those remote areas of Gogrial Diocese. I knew the situation there was dark and difficult, but I kept imagining, if I am running away from them, then what must it feel like for those who are in the actual situation? I asked myself questions like, "Imagine if it were you who was born in that country. Wouldn't you need some people to bring some good news? Can you remember the situation during the Genocide? You were in the same situation. If you abandon these in their desperate need, then you will have forgotten the reason God brought you back to the world after twelve hours of death."[1] Emerging from those questions, I came to a peace that I should go, and God granted me the necessary sign of Dorcus coming to a place of confident agreement.

It was one of the riskiest mission journeys I have ever taken. I knew very well what was happening in the region because my friend Henrik from Germany had recently been imprisoned and almost murdered there. He had explained the complexity of the situation, and the impossibility of navigating all the tribal factions. Nevertheless, I had full joy and peace to go because I knew it was pleasing to God. On the way to the airport, I told my wife, "We know that even if I die, God will take care of everything." When I arrived in Gogrial, I soon recognized that God was working powerfully. The times of gospel preaching were accompanied by physical and emotional healing. There were so many finding freedom from evil spirits, from the bondage of fear, and from other forms of evil that several witchdoctors who were very powerful in the villages saw the hand of God and gave their lives to Jesus. I even got to teach them some practical knowledge like how to filter and purify what little water they had.

Following this wonderful time of ministry, on the long, rough ride between Wau and Juba we encountered a group of rebels.

---

1. The story of God's saving me through the experience of death is told in *Dying in Islam, Rising in Christ*.

The Joy of Sharing in the Suffering of Christ

After stopping us, they asked who I was. I was fortunate that they were speaking in Arabic, which I could follow a bit due to my years as a Muslim imam. Although their Arabic was a different dialect from what I can speak, I could understand the gist. They asked for my identification, and when they saw on my passport that I was Rwandan, they started beating me heavily, claiming that I was a spy. Because the Rwandan government had sent some military peace-keepers to South Sudan, they assumed our government was helping Riek Machal, the president, to fight and suppress them. They switched from Arabic to their local tribal language so that I could not understand anything. I tried to protect my head as they struck me with the butt of their guns and heavy kicks.

When they checked on the driver, they found he was the same tribe as them, and they questioned why he would go with a spy. They shouted, "You betrayed the tribe and you have to die with him!" By this point I had been beaten to the extent that I was no longer feeling pain. Lying on the road, my thoughts went to the disciples who were beaten and harassed, and when they were released from prison, they were overjoyed because they were persecuted for the name of Jesus. I remembered when Stephen was being stoned, he said, "Lord, forgive them." I remembered, too, the many souls that were won for Jesus over the days in Gogrial—a good harvest for the Kingdom—and joy filled me and overflowed. At that moment I was ready to die in joy because I felt I had accomplished the work for which God had sent me.

I started praying, using Arabic so that they might hear my prayer for them. When they heard me committing my life into the Lord's hands and praying that one day they might know and receive Jesus as their Lord and savior, they went aside. They began a heated debate over whether they should really kill us. A few of them were saying that I was following the European way of always using religion as a cover for wrong motives. They eventually agreed that they ought to kill me. With eyes shut, I repeated again, "Lord, receive my soul" and began to speak Psalm 23, "The Lord is my shepherd. I shall not want . . . ."

Part II: Paths to Rediscovering Joy

The one who was to kill me held a gun and a sword. I guess he was still debating with himself what to use for the job at hand. I opened my eyes prepared to meet my master in heaven, when I heard the rumble of a car behind us and the gravelly rasp of halting wheels. I saw the group saluting a high-ranking rebel who had just arrived. They told him that they had found a spy and were just going to kill him. When he stood looking down at me, he said, "This man was just in our village. He was preaching and praying for people. We can't have the blood of pastors on us." He turned on his heel, went back to his truck, and drove off. His word was law, and they decided to leave me, but they took everything I had and left me with only a passport. While the struggle back to safety was bitterly painful, I went overwhelmed with joy that the Lord had spared me for more ministry work. It took months for my many bruises to fade and broken bones to heal, but I had been given a gift that can be received in no other way: the joy of participating in the sufferings of Christ.

While I was recovering in the hospital back home in Rwanda, many asked how I was feeling and others were clearly having to choke down sentiments of "I told you so." Yet through those days I continued to be full of joy, even when I could not lift my arm from the bed. The doctor's prognosis was that I might not walk again, and that they might need to amputate my arm. I was pained for the grief of my wife and for the members of the church who had warned me, but along with the pain I would often feel joy. Whenever they discussed the prospects of what could happen with my situation, I answered, "Praise the Lord that I am still here!" And I kept on reminding them that this is not the only suffering we will meet in the world; instead, I emphasized that it pleased God that I would suffer for doing his work. Overhearing our conversation were other patients in the same room, one of whom was awaiting a risky operation and fearing it might not go well. Hearing what I was saying, he asked, "Would you pray for me to have the courage you have? I'm afraid I'm going to die in the operation." Before praying for him, I shared the word of God from John 16:33: "I have told you this so that in me you may have peace. In the world you will have trouble, but take heart, for I have overcome the world." He was encouraged, and after coming through the surgery well, he healed quickly. He became a strong believer and remains my good friend.

What I hope my experience demonstrates is that enduring affliction for the honor of Jesus brings rewards that are difficult to comprehend but also result in a power that is difficult to deny. If it is hard for Rwandans to accept the risk of suffering for the gospel—and East Africans are well acquainted with suffering—we know the concept is hard for Western Christians to swallow. Perhaps not in theory, but certainly in practice. But it may be that the rewards have not been considered, so we aim now to present them with the transparent desire to awaken more willingness to suffer for Christ. The opportunity may soon be at hand.

A UNIQUE PARTICIPATION IN CHRIST

Many modern Christians have been influenced by a theology of participation in Christ that focuses on Eucharist, or Communion, biblically based on Paul's teaching in 1 Corinthians 10. With roots in the Middle Ages, an elevated view of Communion began to emphasize the worship service of the Lord's Supper as the focal point of our participation in the divine life of Christ. Simultaneous developments in both the Eastern and Western Church turned attention from the death that was signified in the Lord's Supper to the immediacy of the Bread and Wine of the Communion. Suspicion about the knowability of God or the comprehensibility of Scripture, especially by common Christians, resulted in reliance on the visible and tangible. Eating the Body of Christ and drinking his Blood became the focus or even singular expression of connection with God. Sadly for both Eastern and Western Church, this theology destroyed or hid Jesus's own emphasis on participation with him to which the Supper itself actually pointed. As he taught them during the original Last Supper, unity with him and love for him was experienced through obedience, even to the point of death.

A parallel development has occurred in Pentecostal circles and churches influenced by the charismatic movement. Rather than looking to Eucharist as the place of participation, the charismatic movement has turned attention to emotional experience. In this thinking, to *feel* close to Christ is to *be* close to Christ. As every pastor and worship leader has considered, such warm and positive feelings can be encouraged through aesthetic elements of the worship. Whether the space is somber, candle-lit and reverent, with music in a minor key, or exciting with the musical major key and heavy bass, human emotions can be stirred. We are remarkably easy to manipulate. And our affective response according to our preferences tends to spur us to defend our preference as the true and righteous way of approach to God.

Without doubt, much good has come from encouraging emotional connection in worship. We are emotional creatures, and access to our hearts through aesthetics and affective experience should not be ignored. However, access should not be mistaken for the end itself, nor should the outer gate be taken as the place of meeting. If my beloved calls me to come into a room for an intimate talk, it would be a loss if I stopped to marvel at the beautiful doorway or the furnishings of the room, contenting myself with the distant echo of voice when I might enjoy real closeness. But Jesus has been clear that we love him by obedience; we know him by clinging to his words; and we grow in him by walking in the way that he walked—the way of the cross.

Perhaps we should not be surprised that the re-emergent emphases on Eucharist as the essential participation and emotional experience as participation have accompanied the era of ultimate subjectivity in the West and its suspicion of objective truth. The Eucharist experience has the appearance of an objective correction to the full embrace of subjectivity declared by the widespread focus on emotional experience. We hear this note in its defenders' insistence on the objective reality of Eucharist.

Yet, both these emphases ignore both the general thrust of Jesus's teaching and what the Lord of All has explicitly said in his Scriptures. Countless works examining the teachings of Jesus have noted his focus on sacrifice, abandonment into the hands of God, surrender to the ethical demands of the Almighty, and walking the

The Joy of Sharing in the Suffering of Christ

way of the Cross. Dietrich Bonhoeffer's *Cost of Discipleship* may be the best known. Less noted but still prominent is that the teaching of the apostles bears out his focus. In 2 Corinthians 10–12, Paul shares the preeminent assurance of being in Christ: "If anyone is confident that he is Christ's, let him remind himself that just as he is Christ's, so also are we. . . . Are they servants of Christ? I am a better one—I am talking like a madman—with far greater labors, far more imprisonments, with countless beatings, and often near death." He then presents evidences of his extreme suffering and hardship for the Lord's name, which he claims as substantial proof. He concludes with the Lord's word, "'My grace is sufficient for you, for my power is made perfect in weakness.' Therefore I will boast all the more gladly of my weaknesses, so that the power of Christ may rest upon me" (2 Cor. 12:9). Communicating the same idea, Peter draws together the way of Christ and the way of the Christian: "Since Christ suffered in his body, arm yourselves also with the same attitude, because whoever suffers in the body is done with sin" (1 Peter 4:1). And further,

> Dear friends, do not be surprised at the fiery ordeal that has come on you to test you, as though something strange were happening to you. But *rejoice inasmuch as you participate in the sufferings of Christ*, so that you may be overjoyed when his glory is revealed. If you are insulted because of the name of Christ, you are blessed, for the Spirit of glory and of God rests on you. (1 Peter 4:12–14; *our emphasis*)

Both the Apostle to the Gentiles and the Apostle to the Jews agree in commending suffering for belonging to Jesus as the preeminent active participation in Christ. This is not to deny that being part of Christ is an objective reality through trusting in him and receiving his Spirit. That reality is signified in Baptism and celebrated in Communion. And every time we eat the Bread and drink his Cup, we make the memorial of his death and receive the objective grace of our oneness with him in death and resurrection. Notwithstanding, the apostles clearly state that engaging in and participating in Jesus's resurrection life necessarily must bear some resemblance to his own life of perfected obedience.

In his incarnation itself and through his suffering and death, Jesus acted counter to what fallen nature demanded. As the Second Adam restoring humanity, Jesus acted according to heavenly demands and what would be endlessly good—an orientation both supranatural and eternal. Encountering any kind of cost in order to obey God will be blessed by his Spirit because it is aligning with his own heart and mind. The more that the decision or action requires setting aside self-interest and natural comfort in favor of God's interest and eternal reward, the more God's blessing, power, strength, and joy will be given. The apostles agree that the most Christlike way of life, and the life most resembling our pioneer and perfecter, will be tuned by the Spirit and will lead to affliction.

This is what we find in the churches of the global south, where practical theology based on Scripture and the power of the Spirit has yet to succumb to the speculative theology of a comfortable Christendom. Where the everyday hardship of life is more pressing, there is less seduction to live entirely towards the desires of the flesh. Instead, an awareness of the spiritual world and a sensitivity towards its goods help us in the global south to attend to spiritual rewards. Yet, even in Africa, Asia, and Latin America, the rewards of Christ's kingdom are a unique gift for those who sow their strength towards it.

When we speak of eternal rewards, we are necessarily on mysterious ground. As Paul said, "no eye has seen, nor ear heard, nor the heart of man imagined, what God has prepared for those who love him" (1 Cor 2:9). He gives assurance of "the coming ages [wherein] he might show the immeasurable riches of his grace in kindness toward us in Christ Jesus" (Eph 2:7). Although we cannot fully conceive the dimensions and delight of eternity, we do have foretaste of it through the Spirit conveying his delight.

Towards the enjoyment of eternal rewards, Scripture gives us a principle of degrees of glory—"we are being transformed from one degree of glory to another"—and of rewards commensurate with our stewardship. God transforms us as we are no longer conformed to the pattern of the world but have our minds renewed according to the pattern of God. The more we are transformed, the better we are suited to be filled with his glory. In other words, God shapes and enlarges our souls in order to give us more capacity to hold his rewards—chiefly himself. And where he is, there is joy.

When I describe the suffering I have experienced for the sake of Christ, I am trying to convey the mystery of participation in Christ's sufferings. To be beaten because I wanted God to be known is part of Jesus's own experience. To put my life in God's hands without reservation is part of Jesus's own surrender. Through those moments, and uniquely through them, Jesus has communicated part of his own experience to me. We are commanded to have the mind of Christ, but there is a part of his mind that can be known only by enduring suffering for the glory of God. The reason Paul boasts in his sufferings and Peter commends them as true participation is because they bring a joy unlike any other.

CONCLUSION

As we have said throughout this book, joy is a subjective experience. No person can give their joy to another; rather, the joyful person points to the source of joy and encourages others to fellowship with him. In common speech, when we talk of someone having contagious joy, we're really describing people whose lives are fixedly oriented to the kingdom of God and to his glory. They will more regularly feel struck by the joy of the Lord. They will be marked by thankfulness. So their words and their lives point to the way of God and commend it to those around them.

It is common to remark that people who have passed through great suffering for Jesus seem shockingly joyful. If you ask them why, you will hear a common refrain. They cite the privilege of giving special honor to God; they recognize they were sustained in a powerful way by the Spirit; so their lives have taken on the contours of humility and thankfulness.

What you may recognize in that description is the restoration of original design, with which we began this book. In a spiritual sense, suffering for Christ makes a person other-wordly. Through suffering, the world is stripped of its alluring mask, and what is perishing is exposed for what it is. Suffering is not redemptive in the sense that it saves anyone, but for the one who suffers for Christ, his or her life receives a powerful stimulus towards sanctification and the holiness for which we were called.

We were made for God. Until all our other gods are thrown down and all our distorted desires are turned back to God, we will struggle with a sense of inconsistency, futility, and discontent. But when we find ourselves surrendered to the absolute reign of Christ, with his Word ruling in our hearts and governing our decisions, we will increasingly discover that we are at peace. The subjective feeling of that state of peace with God is joy, and nothing breaks the power of our idols like suffering.

QUESTIONS FOR REFLECTION

Although you have not likely been beaten because you took a risk for the kingdom, can you recall a moment when you knew that being faithful to Jesus might have negative consequences. What did you do? How did you feel afterward?

Despite our knowledge that Jesus was the Suffering Servant whose mission was to give his life as a ransom for many, why do you think Western Christians have emphasized positive experiences as participating in Christ?

What do you think is the relationship between a true desire to know Jesus and our attitude towards suffering for his name?

Bibliography

Aristotle. *Nicomachean Ethics*. Translated by David Ross and edited by Lesley Brown. Oxford: Oxford University Press, 2009.

Athanasius. *On the Incarnation*. Translated by John Behr. Yonkers, NY: St. Vladimir's Seminary, 2011.

Augustine. *The City of God*. Translated by Henry Bettenson. New York: Penguin Classics, 2003.

Benjamin, Walter. "On Language as Such and on the Language of Man." In *Reflections: Essays, Aphorisms, and Autobiographical Writings*, edited by Peter Demetz, 314–32. New York: Harcourt Brace, 1978.

Bonhoeffer, Dietrich. *The Cost of Discipleship*. 1937. New York: Simon and Schuster, 2018.

Christian, Jayakumar. *God of the Empty-Handed: Poverty, Power, and the Kingdom of God*. Monrovia, CA: MARC, 1999.

Chrysostom, John. "Homily 76. On Matthew 26.16–18." In *Homilies of John Chrysostom on the Gospel of St. Matthew*. Translated by George Prevost. *Nicene and Post-Nicene Fathers, vol. 10*, edited by Philip Schaff, 456–62. Peabody, MA: Hendrickson, 2004.

Cole, Graham. *God the Peacemaker: How Atonement Brings Shalom*. Downers Grove, IL: IVP, 2009.

Descartes, Rene. *Discourse on Method*. In *Selected Philosophical Writings*, edited by John Cottingham. Cambridge: Cambridge University Press, 1988.

Gilkey, Langdon. *Shantung Compound*. New York: Harper & Row, 1966.

Hooker, Richard. *Laws of Ecclesiastical Polity in Modern English, Vol. 1*, edited by Bradford Littlejohn, et al. Leesburg, VA: Davenant, 2019.

Jenkins, Philip. *The New Faces of Christianity: Believing the Bible in the Global South*. Oxford: Oxford University Press, 2006.

———. *The Next Christendom: The Coming of Global Christianity*. Oxford: Oxford University Press, 2011.

John of Salisbury. *Policraticus*, edited by Cary Nederman. Cambridge Texts in the History of Political Thought. Cambridge: Cambridge University Press, 1990.

Bibliography

Kanana, Cedric, and Benjamin L. Fischer. *Dying in Islam, Rising in Christ.* Boise, ID: Pembroke Street, 2018.

Lewis, C.S. *The Four Loves.* 1960. New York: HarperOne, 2017.

———. *The Great Divorce.* 1946. New York: HarperOne, 2001.

———. *The Problem of Pain.* 1940. New York: HarperOne, 1996.

Freud, Sigmund. *Civilization and Its Discontents.* 1930. New York: WW Norton, 2010.

MacIntyre, Alisdair. *After Virtue: A Study in Moral Theory.* South Bend, IL: University of Notre Dame Press, 1984.

Martin, Alex. "One Diorama at a Time, Miniaturist Reconstructs Aftermaths of 'Lonely Deaths.'" *Japan Times.* Online, November 25, 2019. https://japantimes.co.jp/life/2019/11/25/lifestyle/ lonely-death-reconstructions/

Newman, Tim. "Anxiety in the West: Is it On the Rise?" *Medical News Today.* Online. Wednesday September 5, 2018. https://medicalnewstoday.com/articles/322877

Null, Ashley. "Dr. Ashley Null on Thomas Cranmer." *ACL News.* Sidney: Anglican Church League, 2001. http://acl.asn.au/resources/dr-ashley-null-on-thomas-cranmer/

Olson, Bruce. *Bruchko: The Astonishing True Story of a 19-year-old American—His Capture by the Motilone Indians and His Adventures in Christianizing the Stone Age Tribe.* Lake Mary, FL: Charisma, 2006.

Onshi, Norimitsu. "A Generation in Japan Faces a Lonely Death." *New York Times* Online. November 30, 2017. https://www.nytimes.com/2017/11/30/world/asia/japan-lonely-deaths-the-end.html

Rieff, Philip. *Triumph of the Therapeutic: Uses of Faith After Freud.* 1966. Wilmington, DE: Intercollegiate Studies Institute, 2006.

Shakespeare, William. *The Oxford Shakespeare: Complete Works.* 2nd ed., edited by Stanley Wells and Gary Taylor. Oxford: Oxford University Press, 2005.

Tennant, Timothy C. *Theology in the Context of World Christianity.* Grand Rapids: Zondervan, 2009.

Tolkein, J.R.R. *Beowulf: A Translation and Commentary,* edited by Christopher Tolkein. New York: Mariner, 2015.

Tuchman, Barbara. *A Distant Mirror: The Calamitous 14th Century.* New York: Alfred Knopf, 1978.

Turkle, Sherry. *Alone Together: Why We Expect More from Technology and Less from Each Other.* New York: Basic, 2017.

———. *The Second Self: Computers and the Human Spirit.* Boston: MIT Press, 2005.

World Health Organization. *Depression and Other Common Mental Disorders: Global Health Estimates.* License: CC BY-NC-SA 3.0 IGO. Geneva: World Health Organization; 2017. https://www.who.int/mental_health/management/depression/prevalence_global_health_estimates/en/

www.ingramcontent.com/pod-product-compliance
Lightning Source LLC
Chambersburg PA
CBHW072148160426
43197CB00012B/2300